MEL BAY PRESENTS

WESTERN SWING FIDDLE

BY JOE CARR

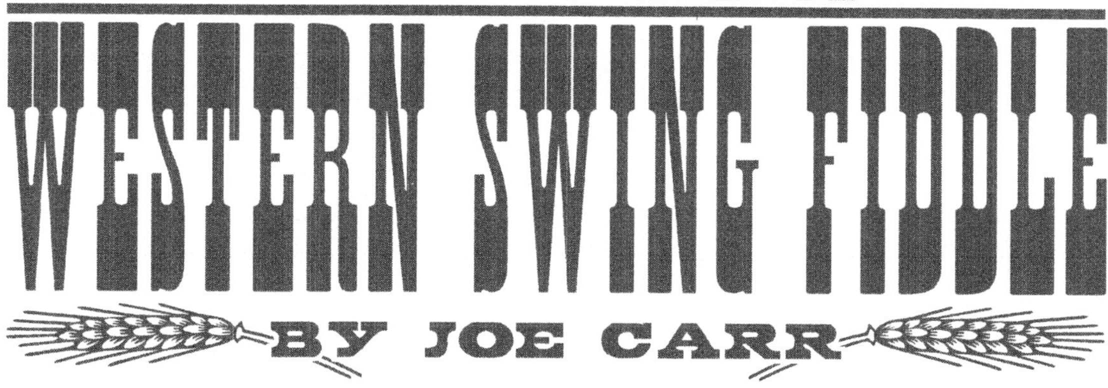

AF334155

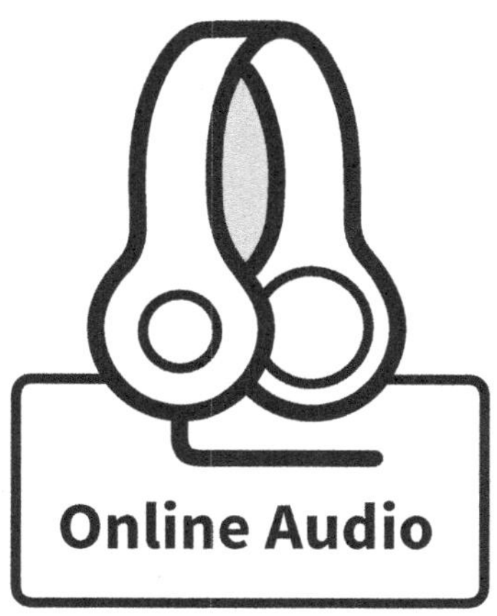

Online Audio

To Access the Online Audio Go To:
www.melbay.com/20289BCDEB

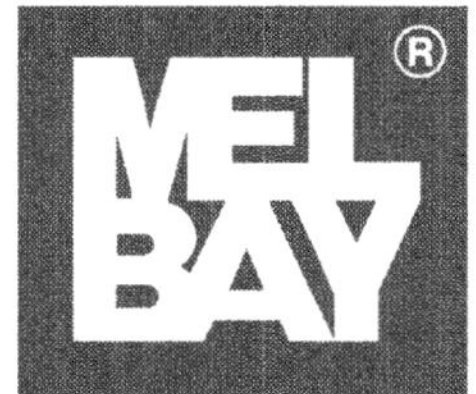

1 2 3 4 5 6 7 8 9 0

Visit us on the Web at www.melbay.com — E-mail us at email@melbay.com

TABLE OF CONTENTS

Preface

About the Author

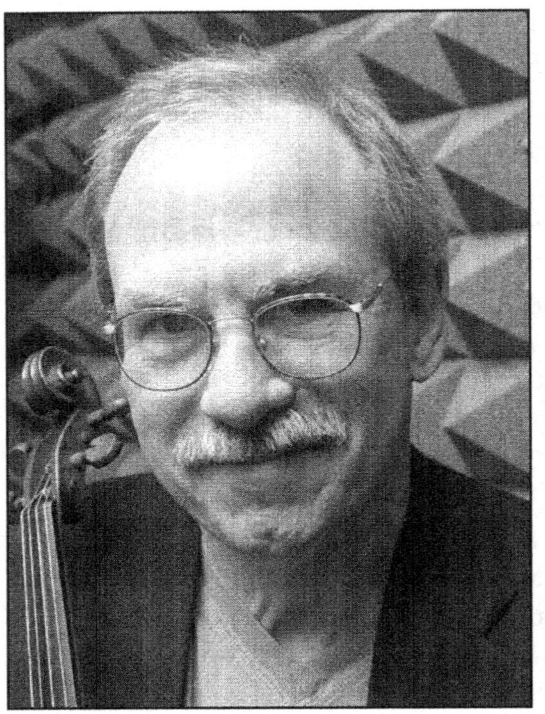

Photo by Wes Underwood

Musicians may not recognize Joe Carr's name at first, but his face may be familiar. That's because he appears in over twenty instructional guitar videos ranging from country to swing, bluegrass and even heavy metal! Add to these his videos on mandolin, fiddle, banjo and ukulele and Joe may be the most recorded video instructor anywhere.

Joe is a self-taught musician originally from Denton, Texas who started guitar at age 13. After six years touring with Alan Munde in the internationally acclaimed bluegrass group COUNTRY GAZETTE, Joe left to join the music faculty in the unique commercial music program at South Plains College in Levelland, Texas.

In addition to two albums on the Flying Fish label, Carr and Munde have published an award winning book about West Texas country music entitled *Prairie Nights to Neon Lights* from the Texas Tech University Press.

Today, in addition to teaching, Joe continues to produce instructional materials for Mel Bay including *First Lessons in Flatpicking Guitar, Western Swing Guitar Styles, Getting Into Flatpicking Guitar, Getting into Country Guitar, Great Mandolin Picking Tunes, Texas Fiddle Favorites for Mandolin* and others. He writes regular columns for *Flatpicking Guitar Magazine* and *Mandolin Magazine*. He is an occasional contributor to *Fiddler Magazine*. He is the editor of the webzine *Mandolin Sessions* at www.mandolinsessions.com.

Acknowledgments

I would like to thank the following people for their help with this project.

Gerald Jones, Tina Carraway, Merna Heersink, Brent Smith and Jean Warren reviewed an early version of this manuscript and made important suggestions, additions and corrections that vastly improved the work. I am honored that these great violinists, fiddlers and good friends shared their time and expertise.

Leigh Taylor's precise editing and layout work made this part of the process easy. Leigh's knowledge of music and attention to detail were invaluable in the completion of this work.

Thanks to Gerald Jones for his tireless work on the CD.

Most importantly, thanks to all the great musicians who inspired this book. It is my hope that this volume will shed some light on the exciting, but sometimes obscure world of improvised swing fiddle.

FIDDLE, n. An instrument to tickle human ears
by friction of a horse's tail on the entrails of a cat.
- Ambrose Bierce (1842 - 1914), The Devil's Dictionary

How To Play Western Swing Fiddle

Music fans everywhere thrill to the sound of hot Western Swing fiddling! From the early bands of Bob Wills, Milton Brown, and Spade Cooley to Asleep at the Wheel and the Hot Club of Cowtown, fiddling is always a central part of this exciting music. Western Swing fiddling comes in three basic styles.

1. Melody:

The melody based and highly stylized approach of Bob Wills' trademark fiddle sound was featured prominently on recordings of "San Antonio Rose," "Faded Love," "Time Changes Everything," "Corrina" and a host of Western Swing standards. This style was not only the cornerstone of western swing, but was a model for much of the commercial country fiddling that appeared in the 1950s and 60s and continues today. This section offers insights into some of the characteristic ornaments of this important country style.

2. Harmony:

Two or three fiddles playing in harmony is the hallmark sound of Western Swing. Nearly every recording by Bob Wills' Texas Playboys features a verse played in harmony by two or more fiddles. This lush sound was likely borrowed from Mexican music traditions. Western Swing recordings in turn influenced other musicians including Hank Thompson, Ray Price and Bluegrass music icon, Bill Monroe, to add multiple fiddles to their bands. Here, we offer some guidance in developing harmony parts to simple melodies.

3. Improvising:

"Hot" or "take-off" style fiddling is a mainstay of Western Swing. To many, "Western Swing fiddle" means the jazzy improvised style heard on so many recordings. Inspired by swing fiddlers such as Joe Venuti, Stuff Smith and Stephane Grapelli, western fiddlers in the 1920s and 1930s established take-off fiddling as an important element in the emerging Western Swing style. Cecil Brower, Cliff Bruner, J.R. Chatwell, Jesse Ashlock and many others blazed a trail followed in the 1940s by Louis Tierney, Joe Holley, Keith Coleman, Johnny Gimble and others. These players, in turn, served as inspiration for modern players including Bob Boatwright, Randy Elmore, Paul Anastacio, Ricky Solomon, Larry Franklin, Ricky Turpin, Jason Roberts, Elana Fremerman ... the list is endless. This section provides a primer for fiddlers and violinists looking for a method to begin or improve their improvising skills. In music, the learning never stops, but you can start the journey here.

"We all have idols. Play like anyone you care about
but try to be yourself while you're doing so."
- B. B. King

Bob Wills Style Fiddle Tunes and Melody

Smith's Reel

Bob Wills is the fiddler most associated with Western Swing. While he organized bands that included some of the best swing fiddlers, Wills never played in the swing style himself. His fiddling style included old time, Texas fiddle tunes and melodic songs played in a very stylized manner. Many of Wills' most famous recordings begin with his trademark melody fiddling, often joined by one or two fiddles playing in harmony.

"Smith's Reel" is a characteristic old time square dance tune which Wills played throughout his career. The second section of the tune begins with a doubled unison A note. This effect is performed by playing both the fourth finger A note on the D string and the open A string together. This produces a bigger sound and was a common effect in Wills' fiddling. Practice scales using the fourth finger to get this unison in tune.

Example 1: Smith's Reel

Track 1

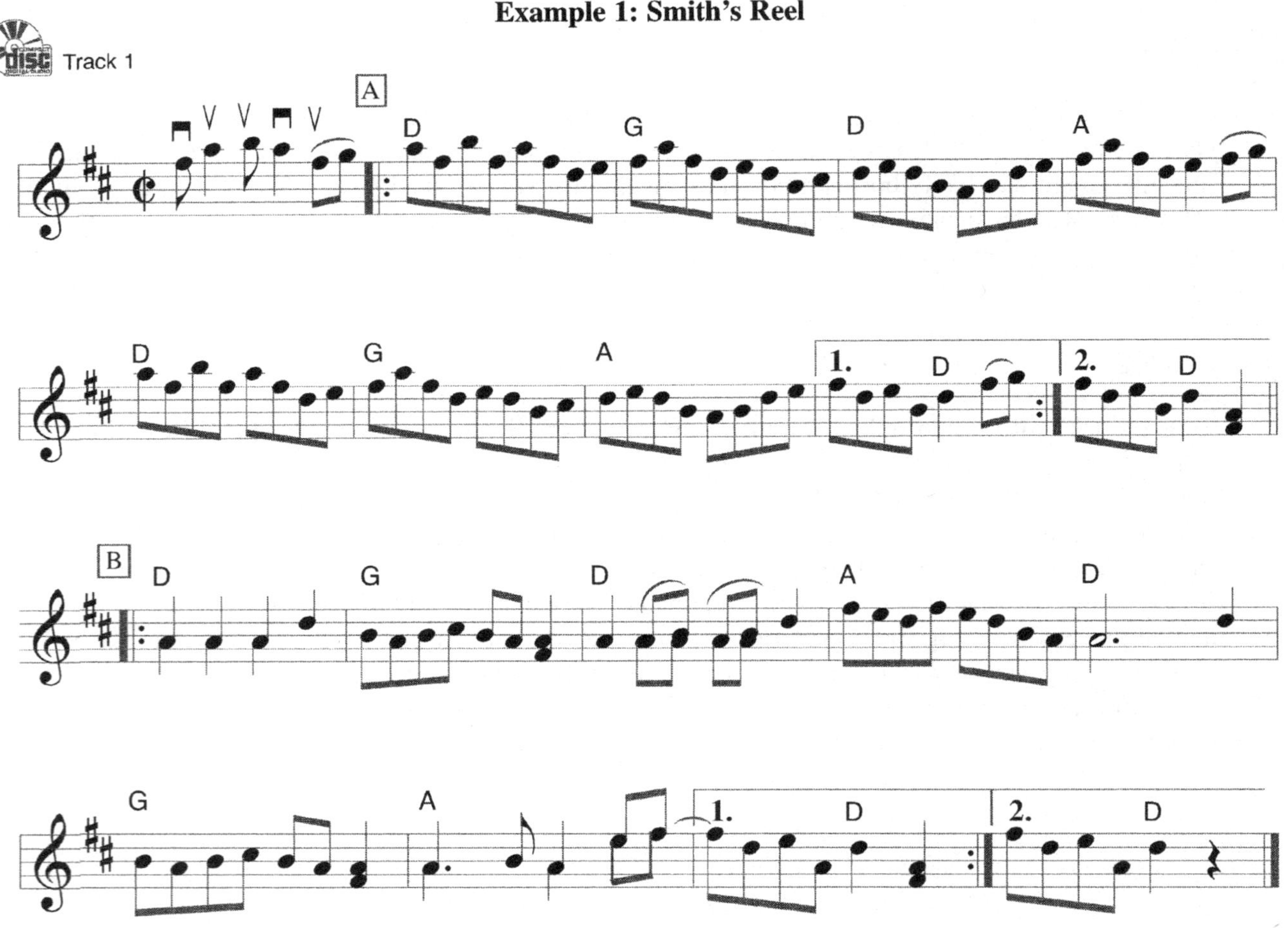

Long A

Here is an untitled old time Texas tune which Wills played on a 1960s country music television show. In his spoken introduction, Wills' only identification of the tune to the band was "long A." This, presumably, was a reference to the type of accompaniment the tune required, that is, the chordal accompaniment begins with a long section (3 measures) of "A" chord. It is another example of what Wills' biographer Charles Townsend called frontier fiddle music.

Example 2: Long A

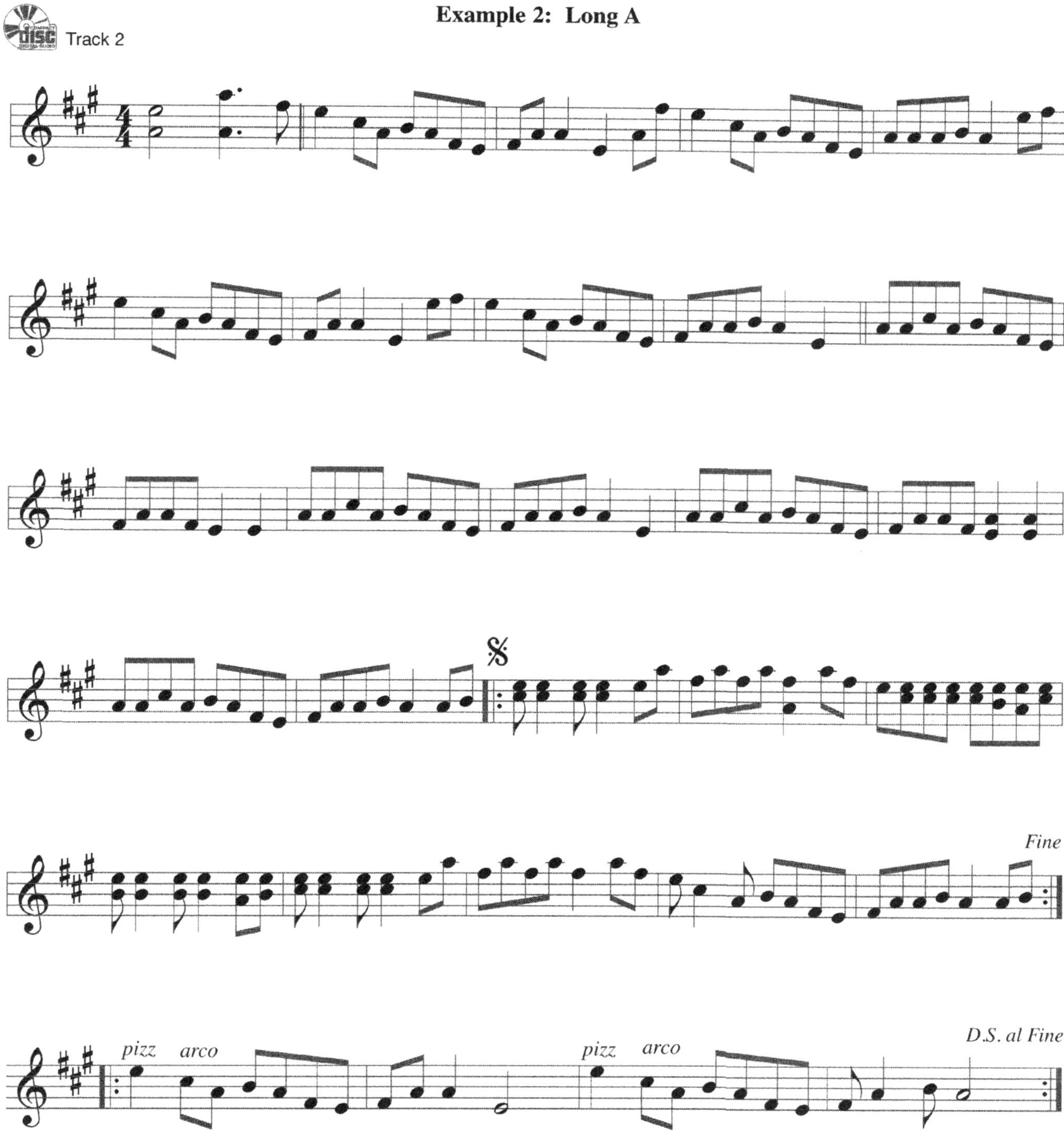

Ida Red

"Ida Red" is an old time tune that Wills often played. This version begins with a common double stop in A that you should learn and practice using the second and fourth fingers. During the first eight bars and in the last two, add the fourth finger "A" drone as much as you like.

Tracks 3 & 4

Example 3: Ida Red

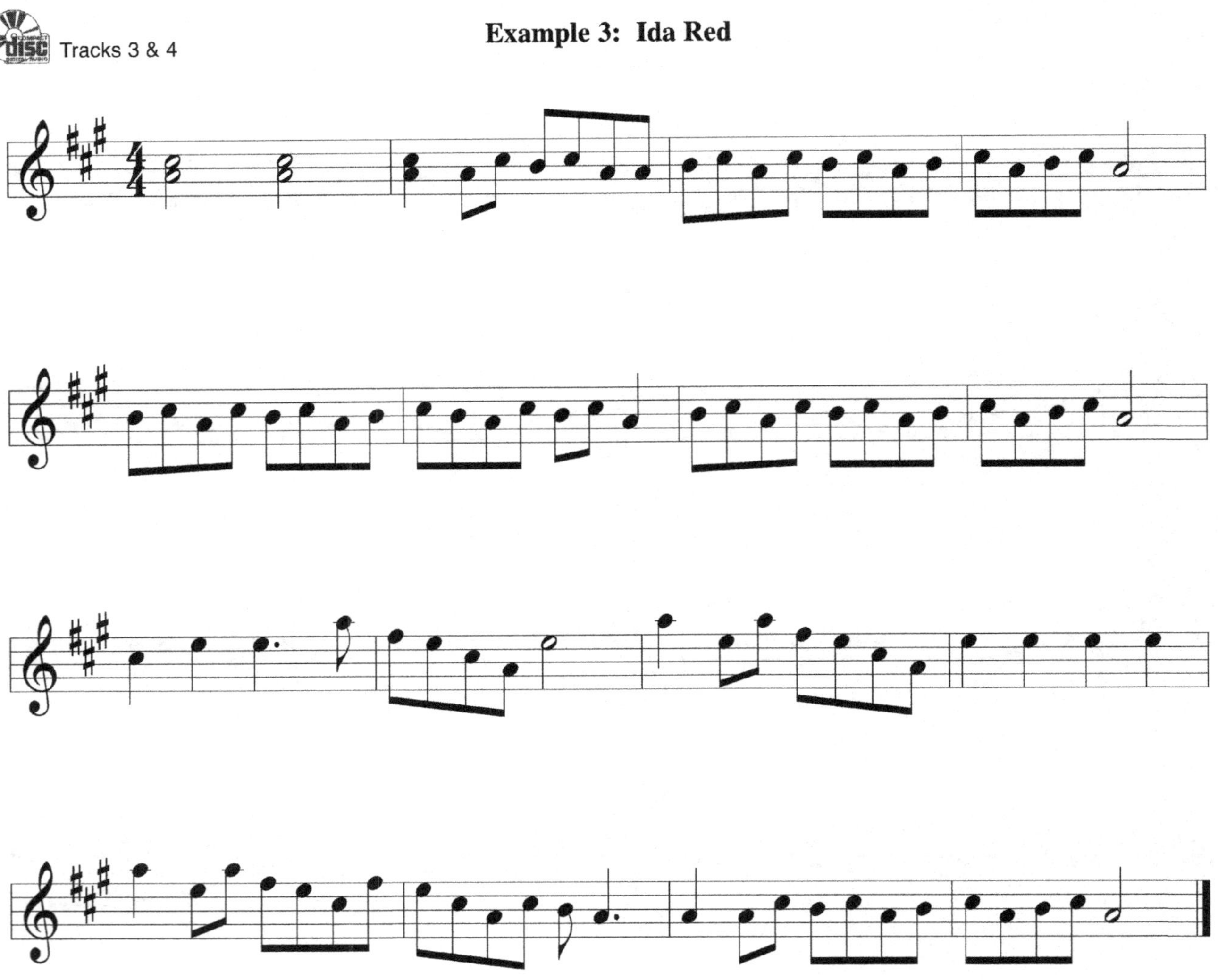

Darling Nellie Gray

"Darling Nellie Gray" is an old song that demonstrates several of Wills' signature moves. Johnny Gimble remembers hearing "Faded Love" for the first time and thinking Wills had started "Nellie Gray." Note the slurred unison in measure 1 to the A from a chord note below. This is a characteristic Wills move which is used later with the open D note. Other characteristic Wills moves include rolling up to a note (measure 3, G note) and drawing onto a note (measure 11, C♯ to D).

Example4: Darling Nellie Gray

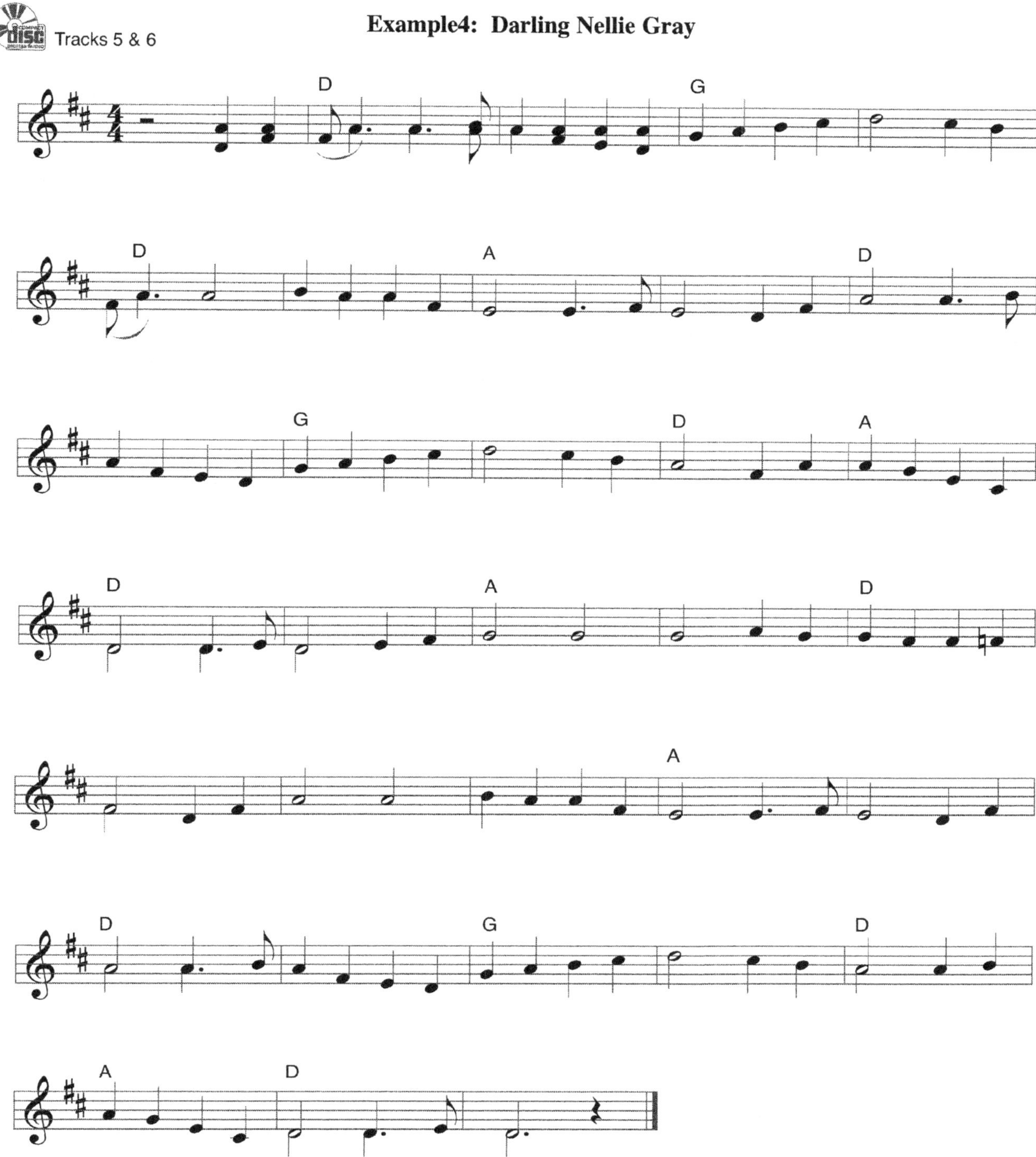

Harmony Fiddling

Two and three part harmony fiddling, sometimes called twin or triple fiddling, is a hallmark of Western Swing. While some fiddlers are naturals at "seconding," (playing harmony parts by ear) the rest of us may need a little help getting started.

When two fiddles play in harmony, one plays the melody while the other plays a harmony part which is often placed an interval of a third above the melody. This part is variously called the "second," or the "tenor" part. There are other harmony combinations, but this is where we will start.

Finding the Tenor Harmony

To begin a harmony part, we need to find a note to start on. While no single rule can explain every harmony situation, the first note of the tenor part is often the next available chord or arpeggio tone above the melody. This will often be the interval of a third above the melody note. To find this note, play the home scale of the song, in an ascending fashion, beginning on the first note of the melody. The first note in the scale above the melody is the interval of a second, while the second note is the interval of a third and so on.

For example, if our first melody note is a "D" and we are in the key of "G," the "E" note is one scale tone above "D." We call this a "second." The F♯ note is the second scale tone above the melody note and we call this a "third."

If our song is in a major key, it is likely that the melody begins on the 1, 3, or 5 note of the first chord of the song. The G arpeggio below contains all the available major chord tones in the first position.

Example 5: G Arpeggio

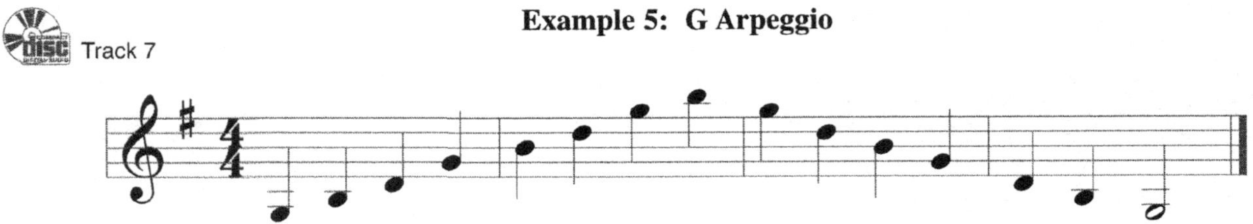

In the next example, the melody begins on a D note. Since we are in the key of G. and the first chord is G, the first tenor note will be the first chord note (or arpeggio note) above the melody note, which is G.

Example 6: First Harmony Note

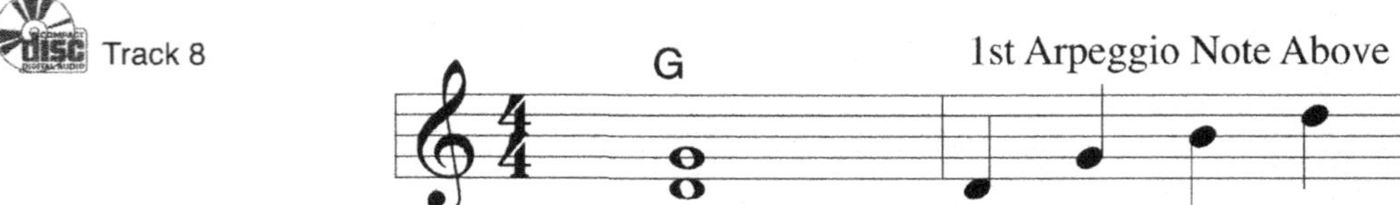

Sometimes, a given section of a song consists solely of notes from the major arpeggio. In this case, the tenor harmony will be one note above the melody in the arpeggio and it will stay in the arpeggio, one note away from the melody. Here is a familiar example.

Notice that when the melody moves to a higher or lower arpeggio note, the tenor part moves to the arpeggio note above the melody.

Example 7: Arpeggio Harmony

Track 9

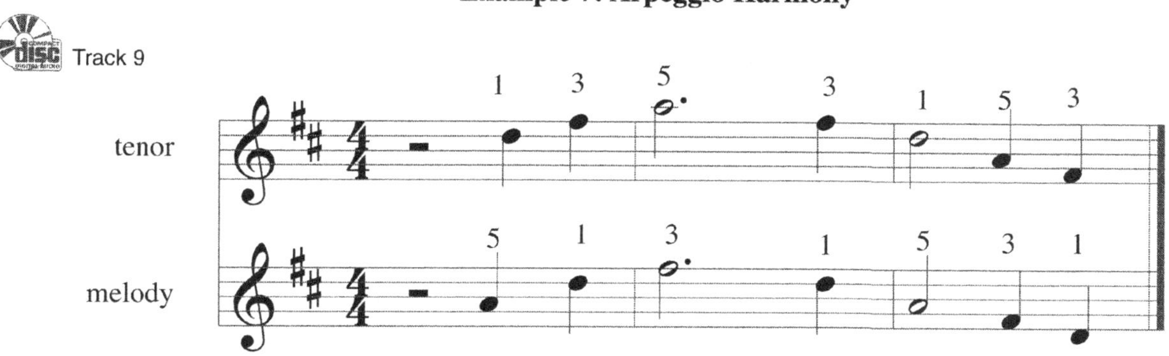

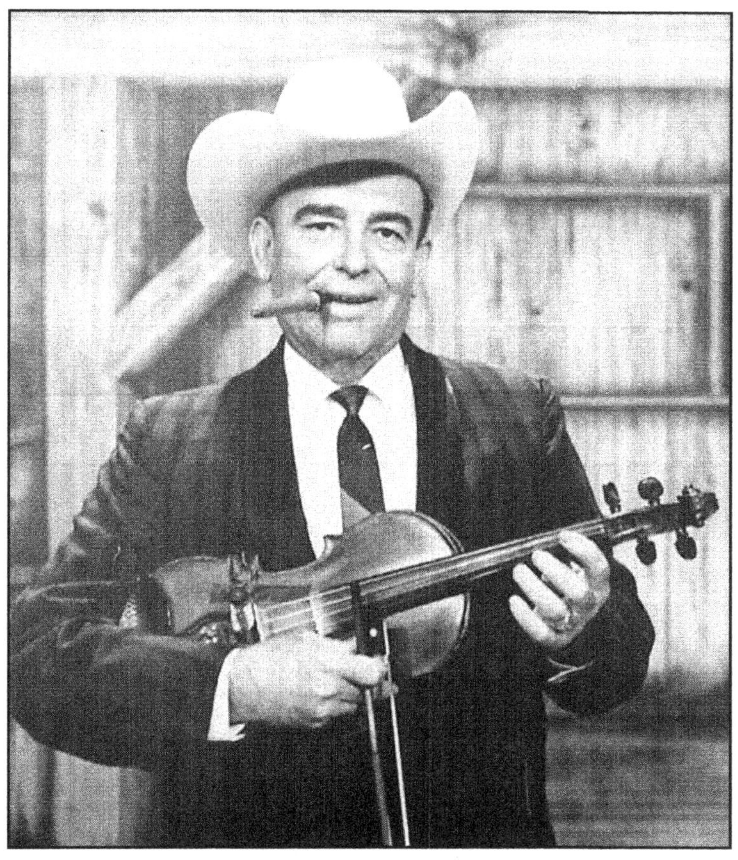

Bob Wills on the set of his KFJZ television program, early 1960s.
Author's collection.

The melody also may move to other major scale tones. In this case, the tenor harmony note is very likely in the major scale and is often the interval of a third above the melody (or two notes higher). The tenor part may not stay a third above the melody throughout a song, however. This can result in a parallel or "chinese" sounding harmony. As the melody changes notes, the tenor part generally changes notes in a scale-like (not parallel) fashion. If the melody moves up one whole step, the tenor harmony might move a half step or a whole step depending on the scale. If, for example, a melody in the key of G begins with this note sequence: G A B (whole step, whole step) the tenor harmony could be: B C D (half step, whole step). This harmony is built on the G scale.

Example 8: Sample Melody with Harmony

Tracks 10, 11 & 12

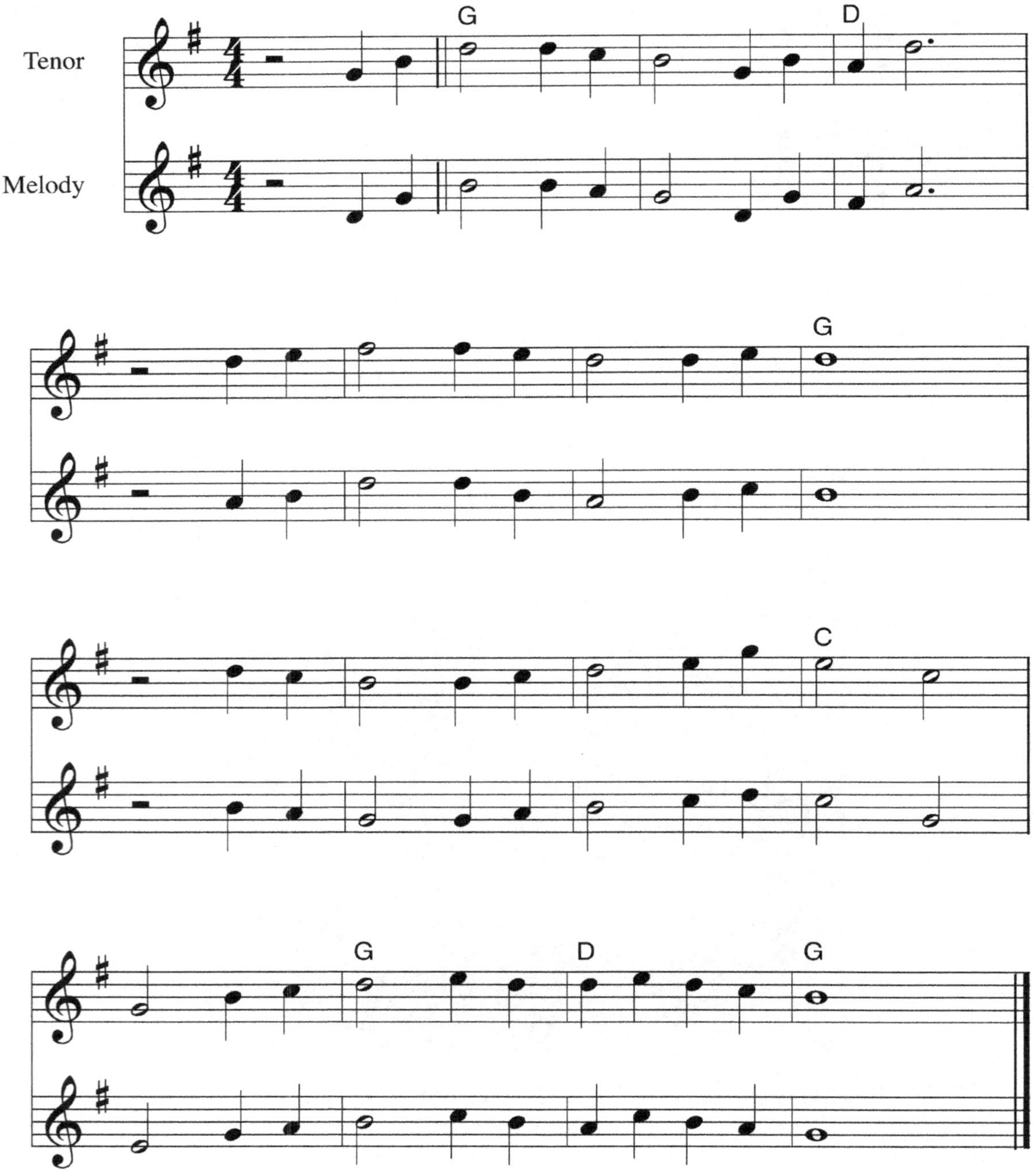

When chords change in a song, the harmony notes generally fit within the current chord even if those notes do not appear in the "home scale." Always keep the chord progression of the song in mind as you work up a harmony part. Example 9 is our sample melody with scale, chord and changing chord harmony.

Example 9: Sample Melody with Adjusted Harmony

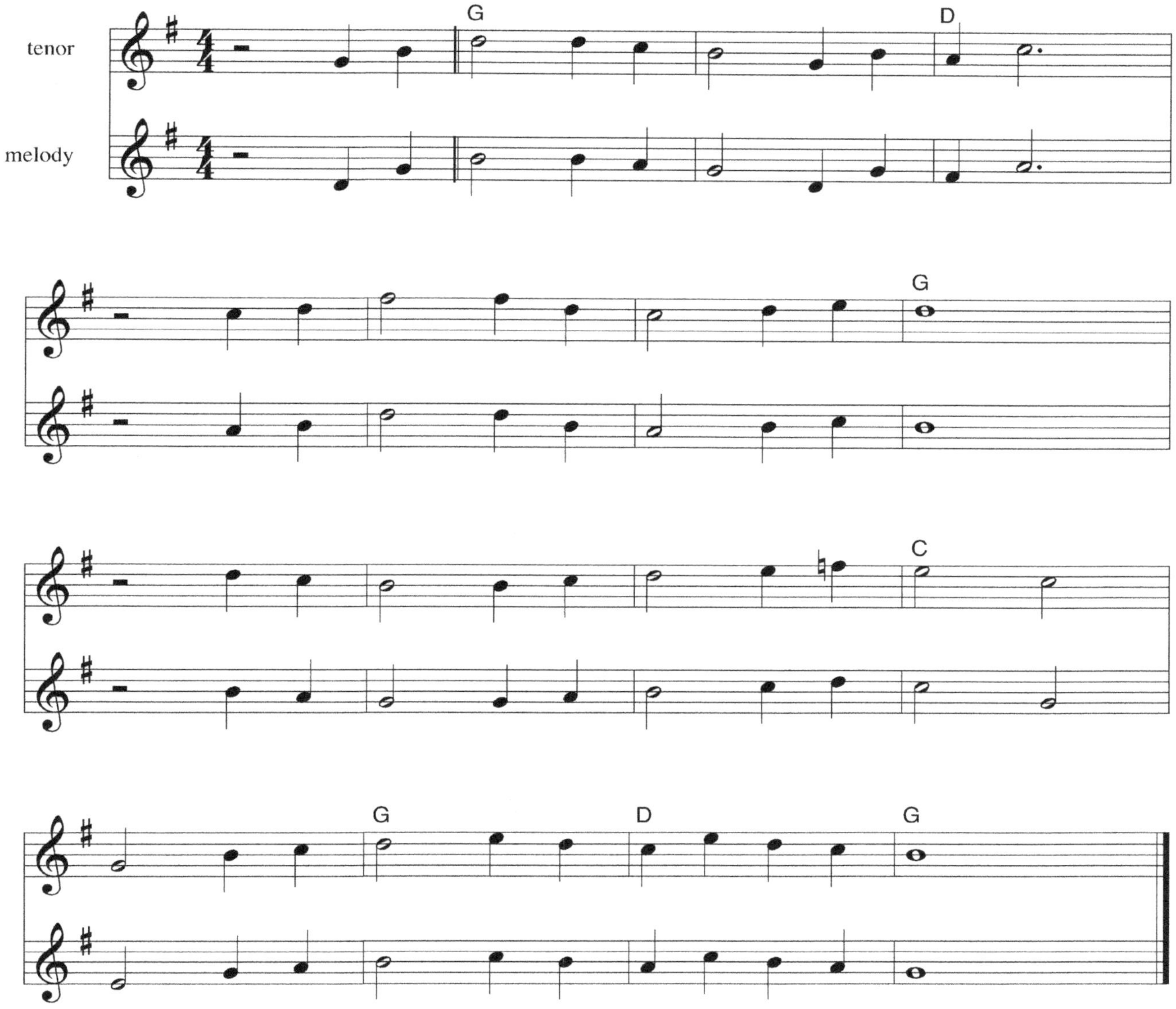

There are two golden rules for an orchestra: start together and finish together.
The public doesn't give a damn what goes on in between.
- Sir Thomas Beecham

13

Example 10 is a two-part arrangement of "Red River Valley." To begin our harmony part, we want the closest chord tone above the melody. The first chord is "G". Major chords consist of the first, third and fifth notes of the major scale. In the G chord. these notes are G, B and D. The first melody note in this arrangement is a "D." The closest chord tone above the D is a G.

The second melody note is "G", also a major chord tone. In the harmony part, we simply play the next available chord note above "G" which is "B". The third melody note is also a chord tone "B," so our harmony note is "D."

You may observe that our harmony part begins the interval of a third above the melody and maintains that interval spacing through the first three notes. Do not assume that harmony is simply always staying a third above the melody!

Example 10: "Red River Valley" - two parts

Tracks 16, 17 & 18

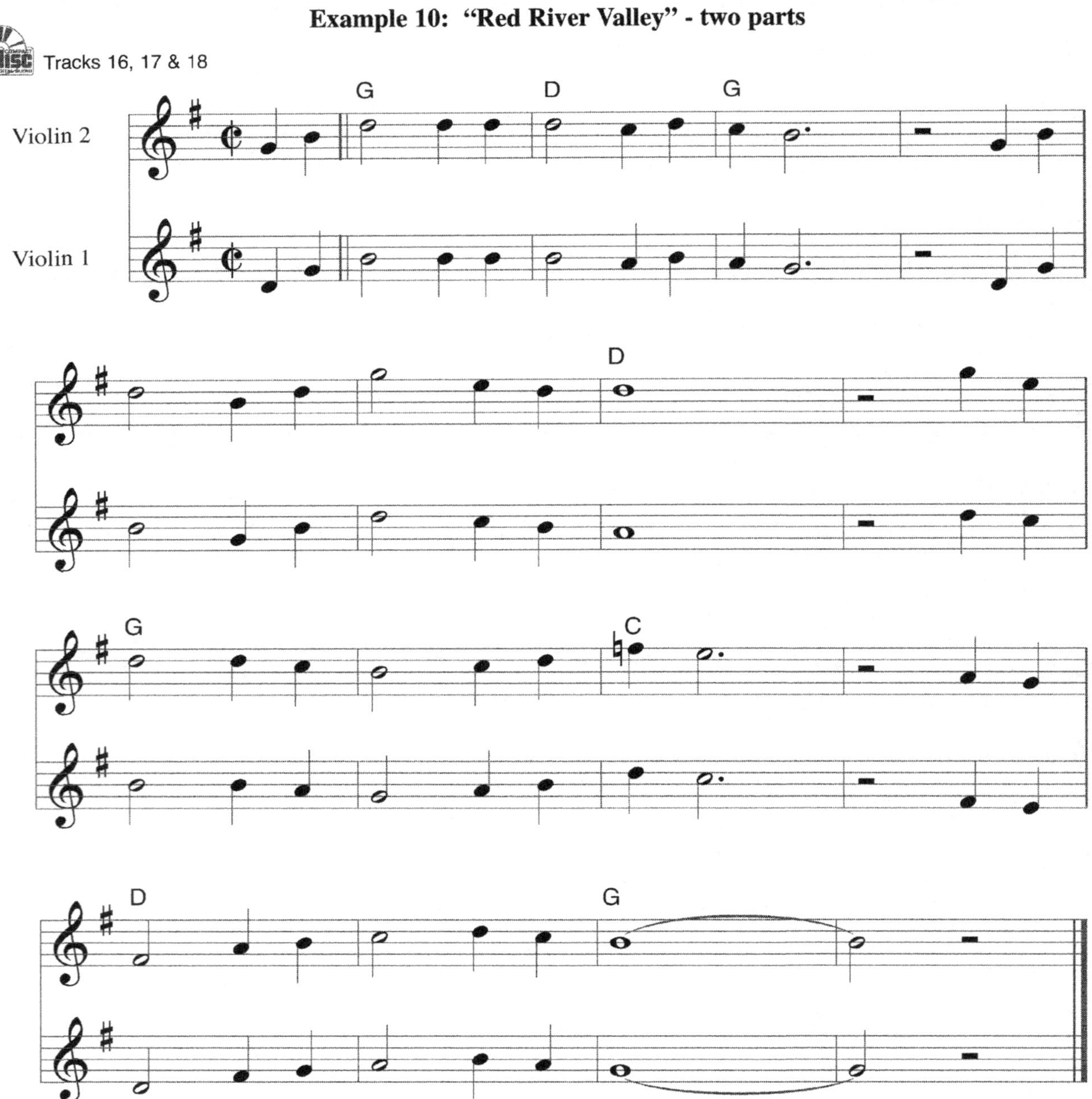

14

Finding the Third or Baritone Part

The third harmony part, also called the baritone, is often placed below the melody so that the melody is sandwiched between the tenor and the baritone. The baritone part generally begins on the 1, 3, or 5 note which is not already taken by the melody or tenor harmony. If the melody begins on a 1 note and the tenor on a 3 above the melody, the baritone would likely be the 5 note below the melody. In the key of G, if the melody note was G, the tenor would be B and the baritone, D.

Example 11 is "Red River Valley" with three parts. The third harmony part begins with B, D and G. Each note completes the G chord, being the third tone in each three note chord. Notice that at each new chord (measures 1, 2, 3, 7, 9, 11, 13 and 15) the three notes spell the current chord. Use the chord changes as points in your harmony part. You can connect these points with other notes from the scale. By trial and error you will eventually get a part that sounds right and does not double any note in the melody or tenor part.

Be aware that sometimes the harmony note may not change even if the melody does or, as in measure three, the baritone harmony may change while the melody remains the same.

Example 11: "Red River Valley" - three parts
Tracks 19, 20 & 21
Violin 1
Violin 2
Violin 3
G
D
G
D
G
C
D
G

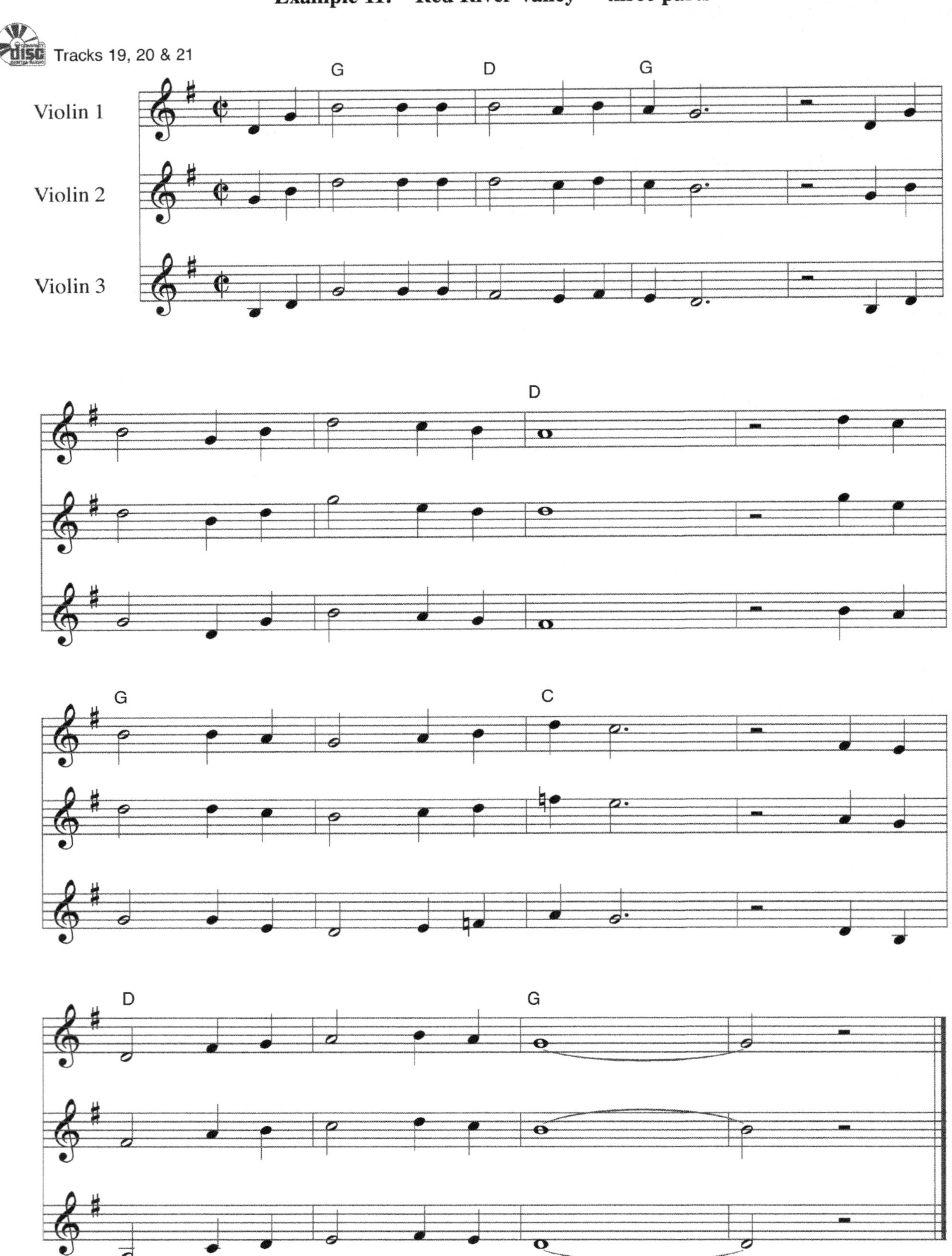

16

In Example 12 our sample melody (Example 8) is arranged for three fiddles. Notice that when the melody and tenor are both on notes of the current chord, the baritone includes the missing note of the triad. The numbers in the music indicate the chord part of the current chord. Thus in measures 3-6, the numbers refer to the D chord rather than G. Notice also the use of the flat 7 tone in measures 3 and 10.

Example 12: Sample Melody - 3 parts

Tracks 22, 23 & 24

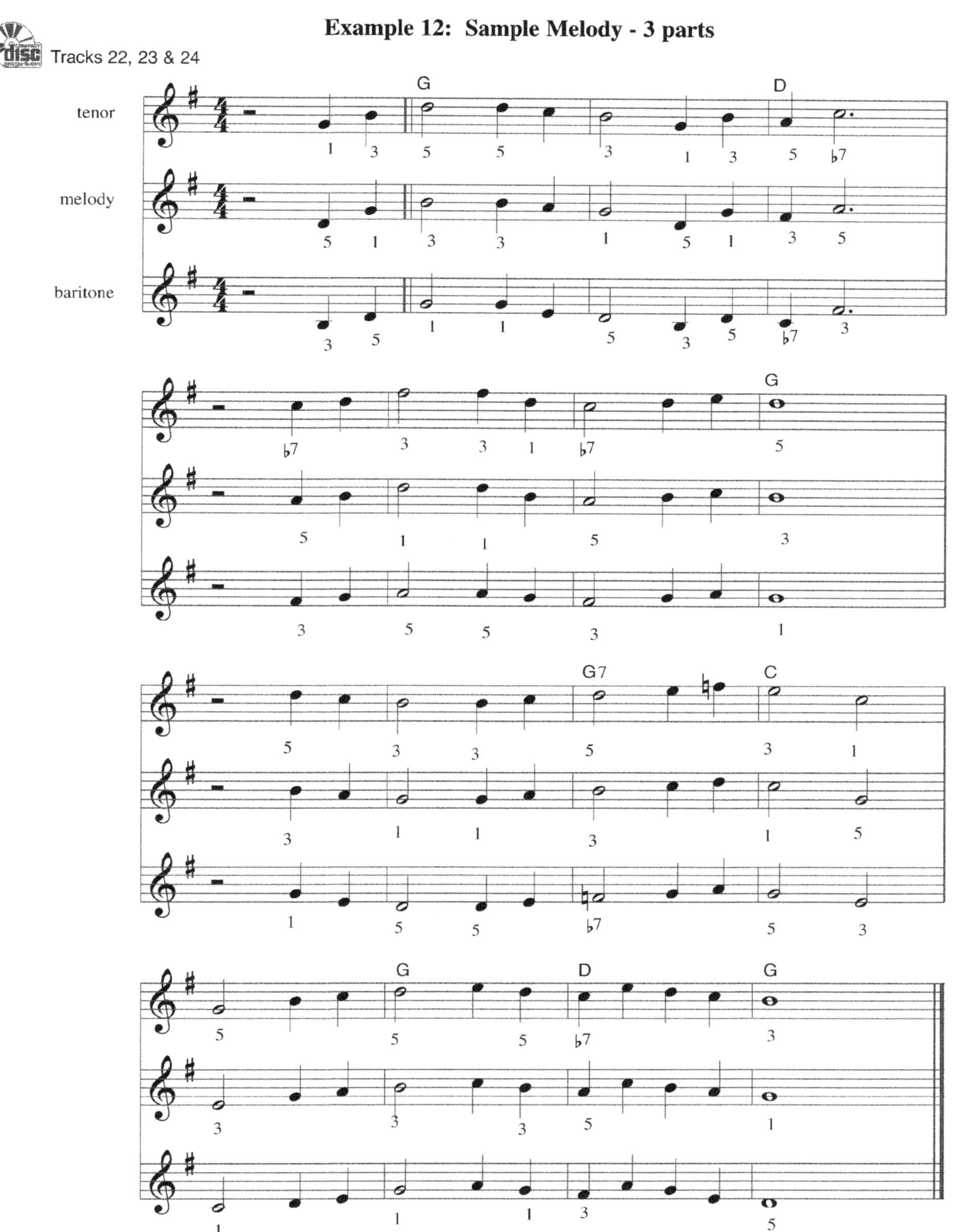

Playing Two Harmony Parts

In some cases the tenor and baritone parts can be played together as double stops on a single violin. The success of this approach depends on the key, the arrangement of the melody, and the skill of the fiddler. Some of the required double stops can be difficult to play in tune. Notice that some small changes are made to the harmony to facilitate playing.

Example 13: "Red River Valley" 3 for 2

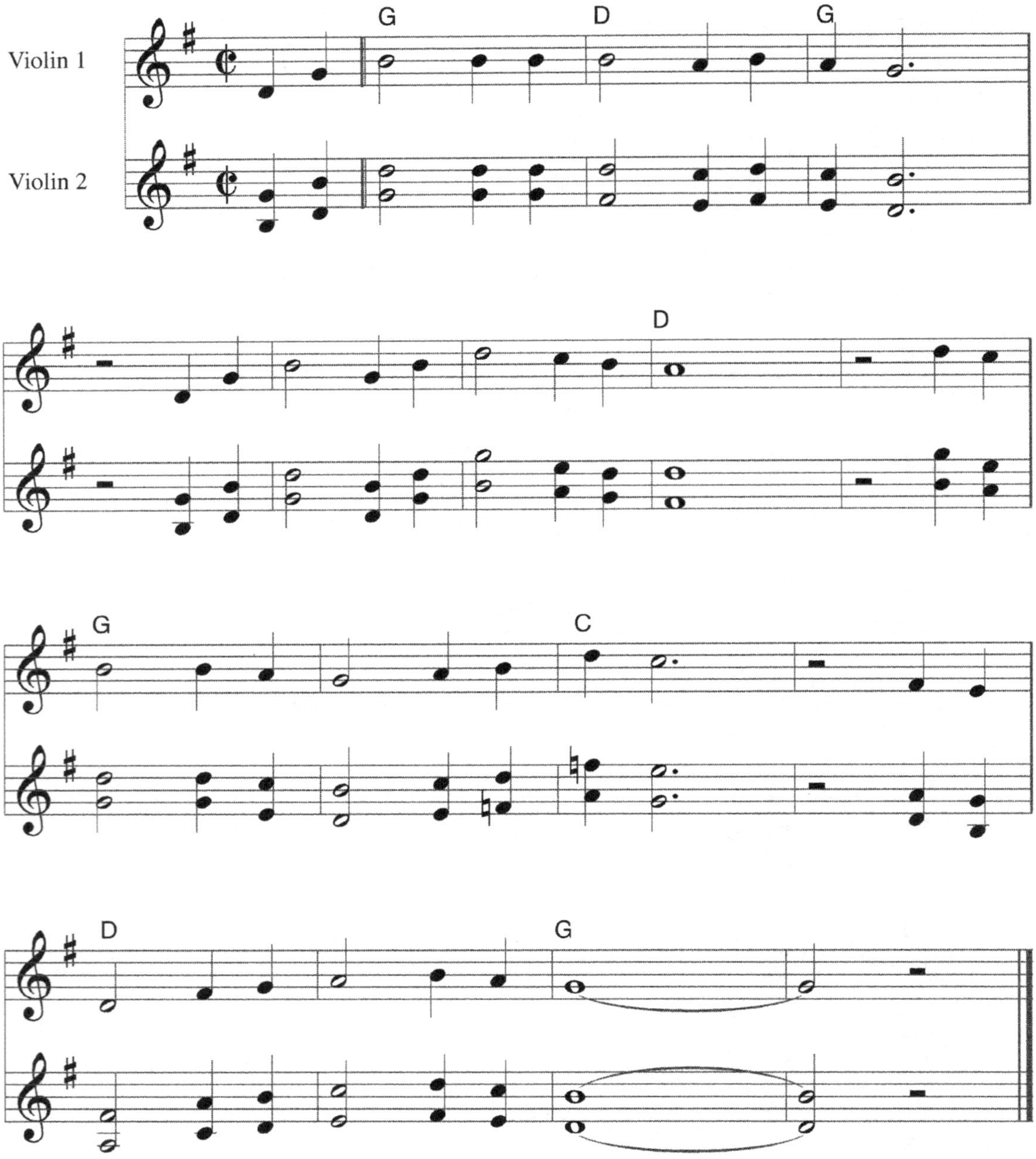

Improvising

Improvising hot, swinging solos is a skill that takes much practice. The process of learning to improvise freely in music is similar to that of learning a new spoken language. The tested method begins with simple conversational phrases that can be used in common situations. Later, as you become more comfortable, more complex situations are introduced that require increasingly complex responses. Each new musical lick you learn is like a new word or phrase in this new language. At first, you simply repeat what you hear. Later you will be able to "say" new interesting things, combining the "words" in new ways and you will be finding your own unique musical voice. The great improvisers speak "music" as freely and spontaneously as we speak our native languages. It is a skill to be admired and the goal towards which we all strive. Listen regularly to improvised music.

You Must Know The Chords

Western Swing music is based on relatively simple chord progressions. As fiddlers, we must know the key of the song and the chord progression in order to solo effectively. Fiddlers often have limited chord knowledge and therefore have difficulty with this part of learning to improvise. You may want to learn some chords on the guitar or mandolin to help get a better understanding of how progressions work. This section contains all the scale, chord and progression information you need to get started.

How To Approach This Material

Continuing with the language analogy, your first improvisations should be like conversations. Don't concern yourself with the theory at first, just have some fun playing these examples with the CD tracks. Don't worry if you don't fully understand the "theory" of the music. Play with the CD track, memorize the new licks and try to incorporate it into your own original solo. As you play with the track, experiment to find how many places a lick will and won't work. You will be able to absorb the actual music more quickly than the theory. After you have played the phrases for some time and have "made it your own," study the theory material. When you understand the theory of the lick, you'll be able to use it in other keys and in new situations.

It is very important that you experiment with these new sounds by playing with the CD. Beginning improvisers are shy and are super-critical of their first attempts. This is counter-productive! Just play and listen to yourself. When you play notes you like, remember them. When you play unpleasant notes, remember those too. Don't worry if your solos sound trite or dumb to you. We all have to crawl before we can walk.

Improvising Strategy One: Playing One Scale or Pattern for an Entire Chord Progression

Beginning improvisers often use a single scale or pattern which works for all the chords in a progression. We will learn three scales in the key of G which can be used for this approach: the Major Pentatonic Scale, the Major Scale, and the Blues Scale. Each scale has its own sound and when used alone, each has strengths and weaknesses. Later we will combine these scale types to create more complete solos, but for now let's get playing!

1. Major Pentatonic Scales

The quickest way to start soloing is to use the five note major pentatonic scale. What is a pentatonic scale? The familiar major do-re-mi scale has eight notes. The fourth and seventh notes of the major scale can be problematic in a progression, if they are used incorrectly. In other words, these two notes are the most likely to sound wrong if they are played at an inappropriate time. With the five note major pentatonic scale, we eliminate these two notes and have the freedom to start soloing with a minimum of preparation.

Here is the G major scale followed by the major pentatonic scale. Notice the pentatonic scale is missing the C (4) and F♯ (7) notes. Practice this scale until you see it as a shape or finger pattern on the fingerboard. Memorize it as a pattern, not as a series of notes. The finger pattern from the G string to the E string is: 012 013 013 0234. Play the scale up and down until the sound of each successive note is no longer a surprise. Try to hear the pitch of each new note before you play it. Some players describe this scale as having an oriental or Native American sound.

Example 14: The G major scale and the G major pentatonic scale

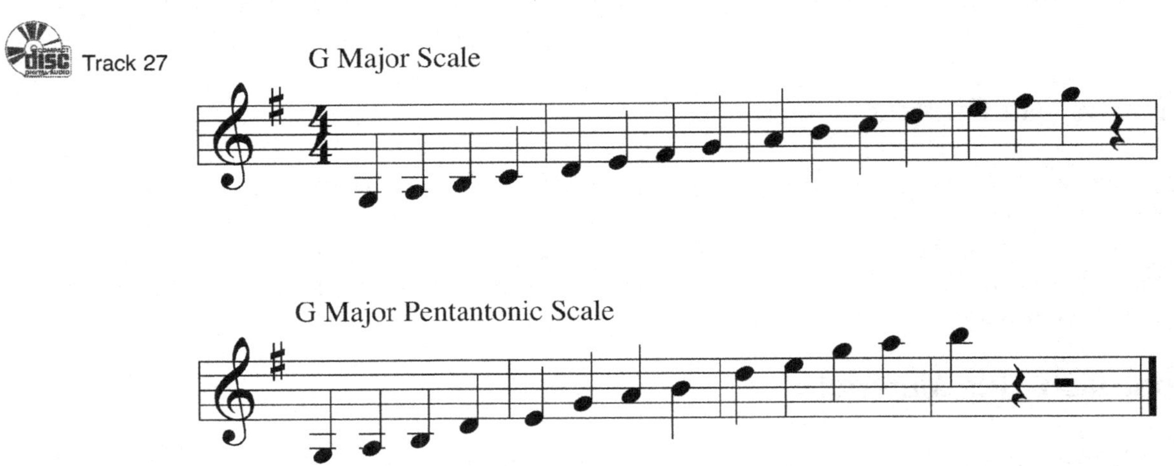

The next CD track uses "Call and Response" to develop your ear. The fiddle plays a lick on the track and then rests for you to repeat. Below I have written out the first three "calls." The remaining licks are not written so that you will develop your ear. This may be difficult at first, but keep trying. This ear training is very important for improvisers.

Example 15: Major Pentatonic Call and response

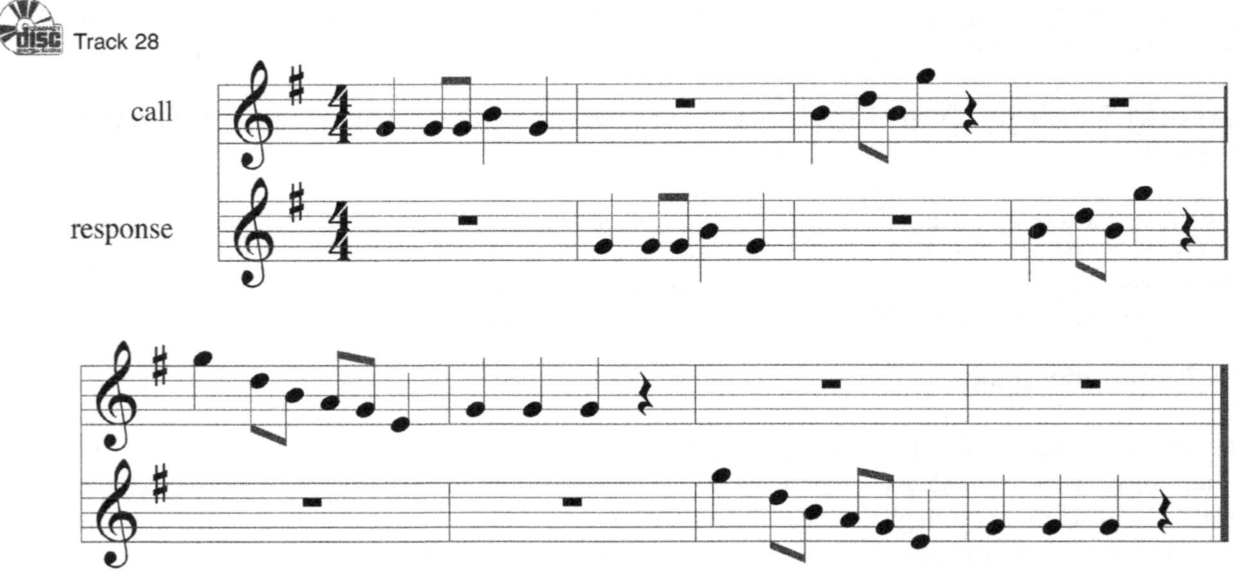

You can play G major pentatonic licks every time a G chord occurs in a song. More importantly, you can play this scale over all three chords of a G blues progression. We will learn about the theory later. For now, play the following solo with the fiddle on the CD track. The first time through the solo there are no chord changes, followed by the solo with the progression. When you are comfortable, try playing with the track using the notes of the scale in any rhythm or order you choose

Example 16: Major pentatonic solo with and without chord progressions

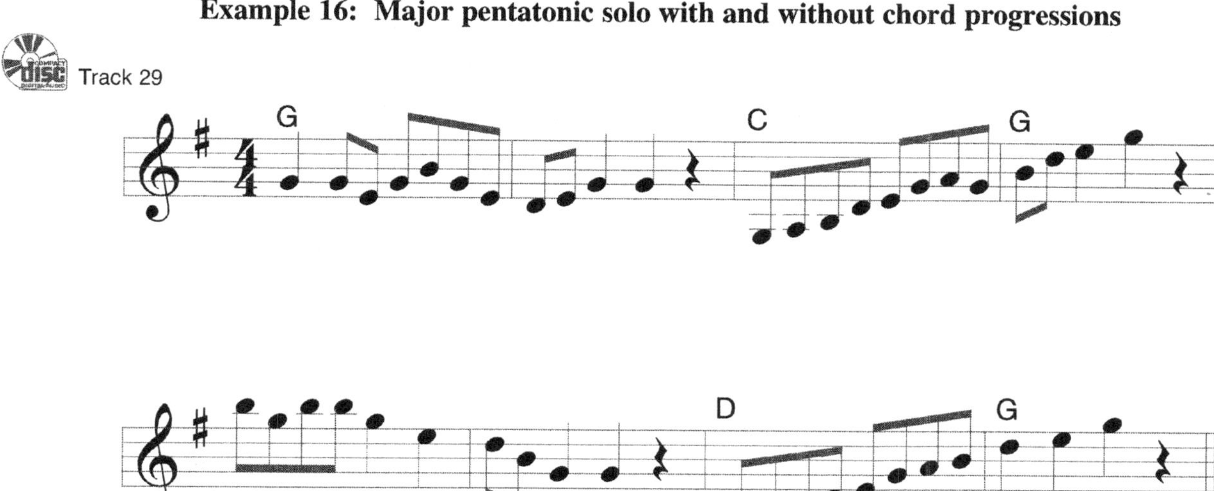

Notice that even though the chords change, we continue to play the G major pentatonic scale.

Joe's Soloing Rule #1   For two and three chord songs (1, 4, 5) find the key and use that major pentatonic scale.

Why It Works   The G pentatonic scale contains the notes G, A, B, D, and E. These notes also appear in the C and D scales. You can solo freely with this pattern knowing you can't go wrong. There are no wrong notes! This will work with many two and three chord Western Swing songs including: "Faded Love", "Stay All Night", "Time Changes Everything", "Ida Red", "Corrina, Corrina" and "Milk Cow Blues".

This is a powerful bit of information. Many good players use this idea exclusively when they make up solos. Of course, you need to know the major pentatonic scale of every key in which you plan to play. These are listed in Appendix #1.

Continue your study of pentatonic scales by selecting different keys from the appendix. Try them out using the practice tracks on the CD in the appropriate key. You can use these same tracks to try out different ideas throughout the book.

2. Major Scales

Solos based solely on pentatonic scales seem to drift above the chords. They never give the listener a sense of the chords that are changing. This is why pentatonics are a great survival tool when you don't know the song you are playing.

To better fit the progression however, we need notes from the entire major scale. We also need the full major scale to find the melody of most songs. You should become familiar with all the first position major scale fingerings (Appendix 2). While scales are not music, they contain the notes from which we build solos. The arpeggios, licks, and phrases can be found in the scale patterns. Memorize the G major scale.

Example 17: G major scale

G MAJOR SCALE

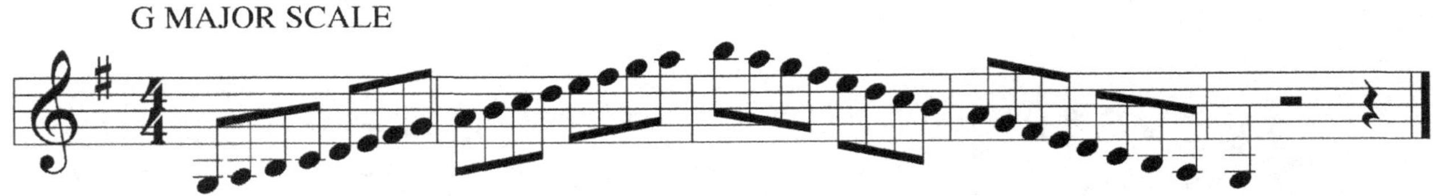

Example 18 shows a solo based on the major scale over a progression like the pentatonic solo. Notice I am careful not to linger on the four note (C) during the G chord. I also avoid the seven (F♯) during the C chord.

Example 18: G Major scale solo

Scale Patterns

Scale patterns are useful soloing tools that can be used with any scale type. Here are two major scale patterns followed by "licks" that use these patterns.

Example 19: Scale Patterns, I

Track 33

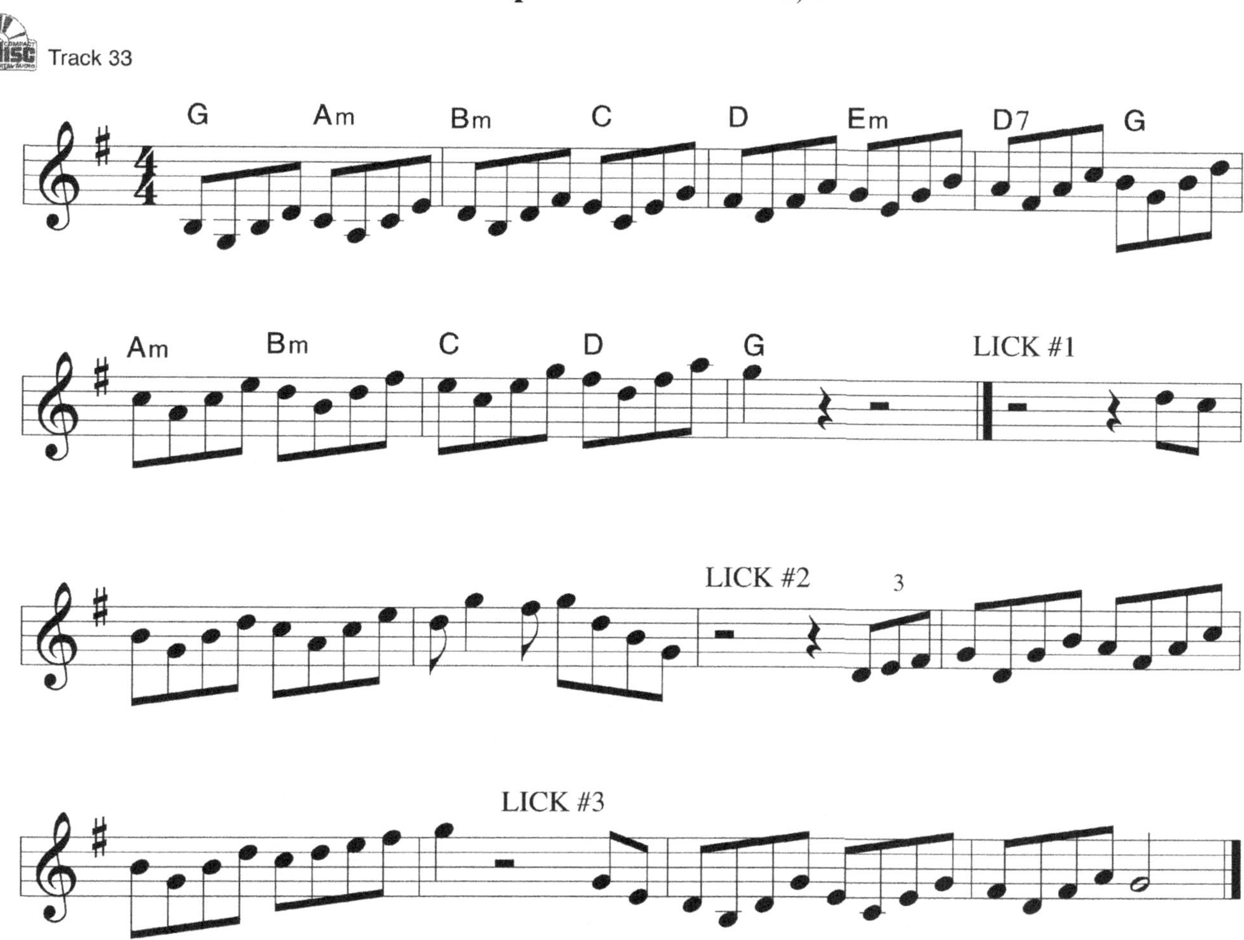

Is it not strange that sheep's guts should hale souls out of men's bodies?
-William Shakespeare

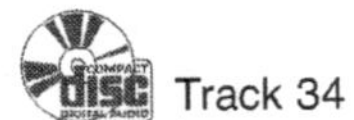

Example 20: Scale Pattern, II

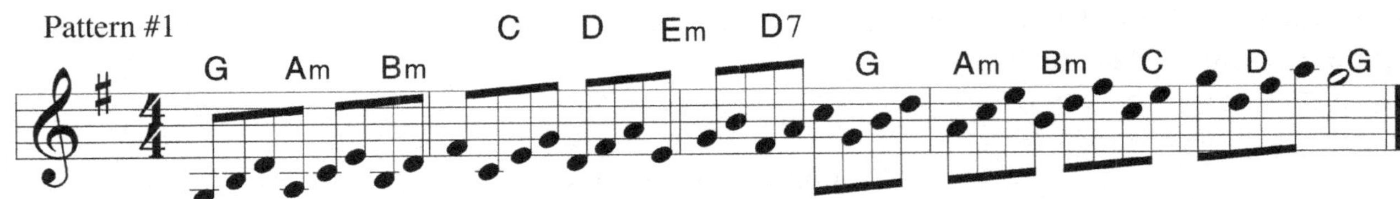

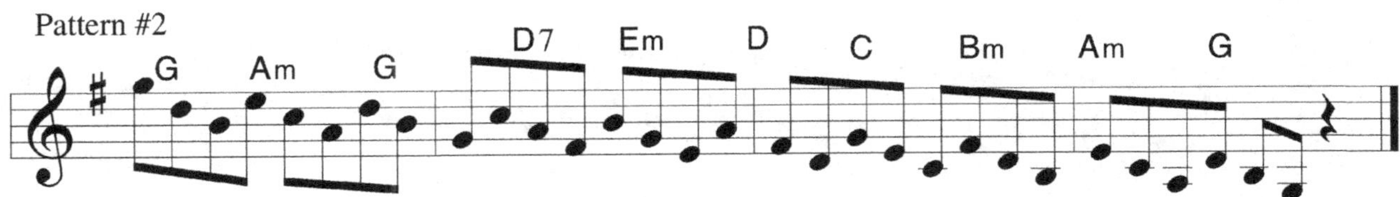

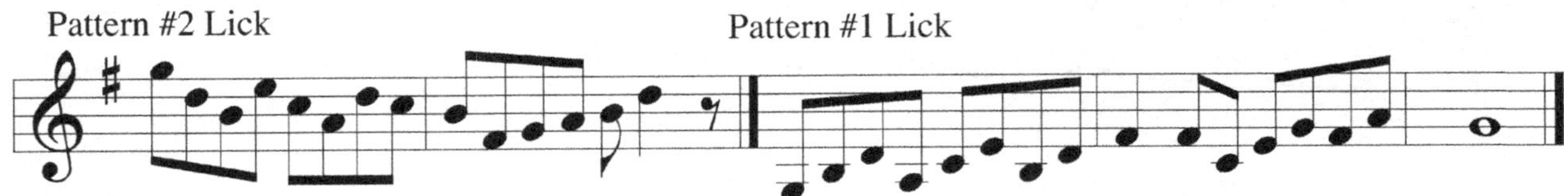

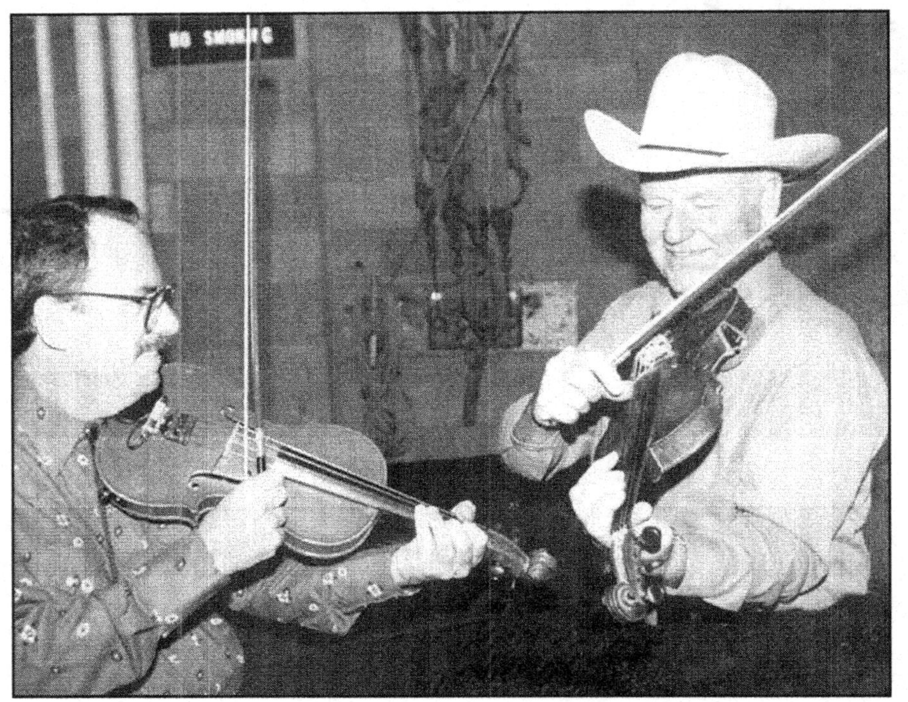

Joe Carr and Johnny Gimble
Author's Collection

Chord arpeggios are great building blocks for solos. Chords are typically described as having three or more notes, however on the fiddle we are generally limited to two notes at a time. An arpeggio is simply the notes of a chord played individually, often in ascending or descending order. A major chord (or arpeggio) consists of the first, third and fifth note of the major scale. We can start or end on any note of the chord. Memorize the G arpeggio shown below.

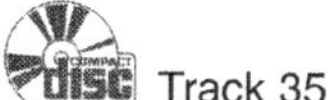

Example 21: G major arpeggio

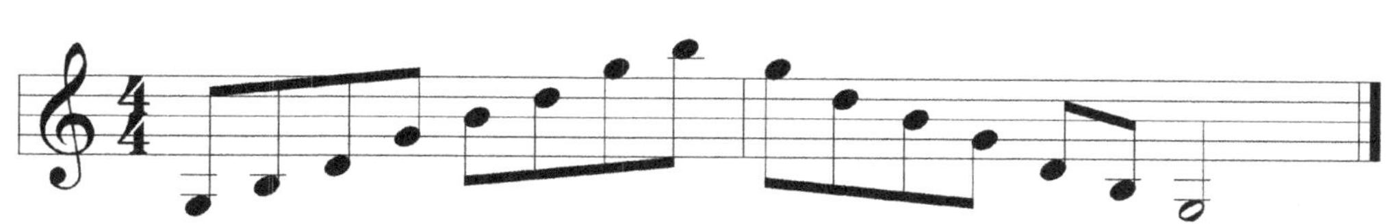

The next example combines the G major scale and arpeggio to create solo material. Play through the solo below and notice how the notes fit the accompaniment on the CD.

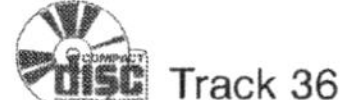

Example 22: Scale and Arpeggio Solo

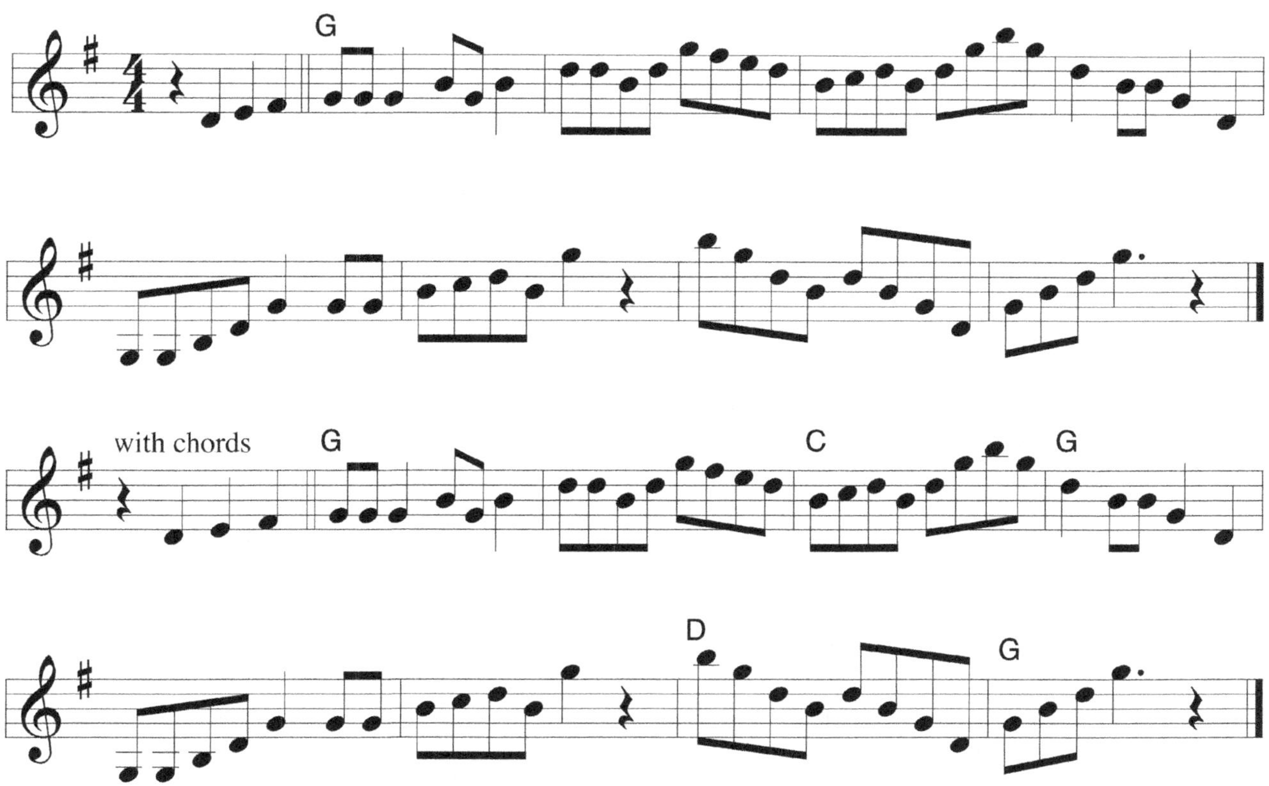

Notice that as with the pentatonic scale, the chords change, we don't. And it sounded pretty good. There are musical reasons why it worked better sometimes than others, but for now, just notice that it generally sounded good.

Joe's Soloing Rule #2   Find the key the song is in and play notes from that major scale and arpeggio.

Why It Works   The G, C and D chords are built on the 1st (G), 4th (C), and 5th (D) notes of the scale. These scales have many notes in common with each other and only a few different.

```
G scale (one ♯)        G A B  C D  E F♯  G A B C  D
C scale (no ♯ or ♭)           C D  E F   G A B C  D
D scale (two ♯'s)             D  E F♯  G A B C♯ D
```

The three scales are the same except for the F and C notes.

Create your solo from the major scale and arpeggio, and ignore the chord changes. This will not work in all situations or with all songs, but it is a good place to start.

Once you are comfortable playing the written solo, try changing the solo a few notes at a time. Perhaps you could change only the rhythm on the first time through the progression. Then experiment with parts of the G scale or bits of the arpeggio. Don't be afraid to make mistakes. If you play a wrong note, remember what and where it was and avoid it on your next try.

Other Major Scale Applications

You now have three tools to use in creating a solo over a simple progression: 1) the pentatonic scale, 2) the major scale and 3) the arpeggio. These three approaches have other important uses.

The major scale can be used to solo over any chord derived from the harmonized major scale.

The chords derived from the major scale are 1, 2 minor, 3 minor, 4, 5, 6 minor, and 7m7♭5. In the key of G these would be: G, Am, Bm, C, D, Em, and F♯m♭5. This means that if a song is in the key of G and it only contains the above listed chords, you can solo freely using just the notes from the major scale!

The 1 chord and the 6 minor chord share the same scale. The major scale is also the natural minor scale of the 6 minor chord. In other words, a G major scale is also an E natural minor scale. This is more obvious when the G scale is played from E to E.

When a minor chord appears in a song, the relative major scale of the minor chord can be used. See Appendix 5 for a complete list of relative majors and minors.

 Track 37

Example 23: E Natural Minor

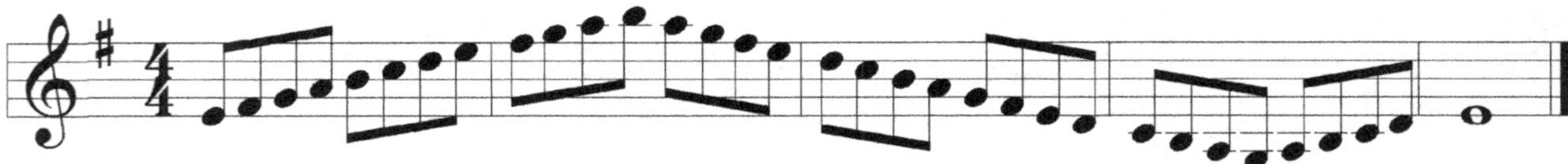

A number of Western Swing songs have a section in which there is little or no chord movement. "Ida Red" (key of A) and the verse of "Stay All Night," (key of G) are examples. Although there may be a quick 5 chord in the last measure of each 4 bar phase, the soloist often plays as if the song simply stays in one chord.

In the next example, we play the same eight measure melody over two sets of chords. The CD track repeats this progression four times (32 measures) for practice.

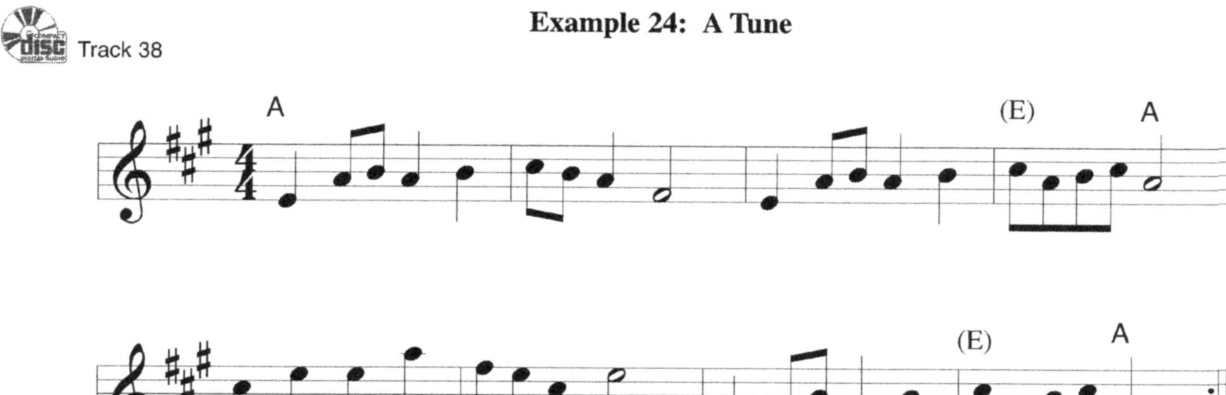

Example 24: A Tune

3. The Blues Scale

The sound of the blues is an important element of Western Swing fiddling. There are many different versions of this scale but they all generally include these tones: 1, ♭3, 4, 5, ♭7. In addition, the flat 3 may be raised to a major 3 and the 4 may be raised to a sharp 4 (also called the "flat 5"). Here is the complete scale in G.

Example 25: Blues Scale

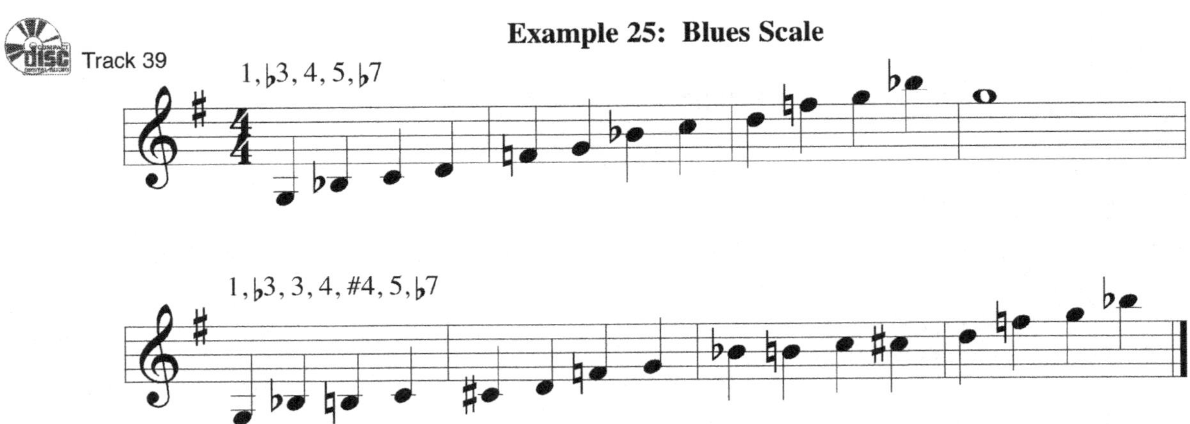

The blues scale can be used the same way we have used the major pentatonic, the major scale and major arpeggio. Notice in the following example how the flatted (minor) third is sometimes raised to the major third. This slide releases the tension caused when a minor third in the lead is played with a major third in the rhythm.

These four approaches can be combined in any fashion to produce solo material.

> **Joe's Soloing Rule #2**   Find the key the song and play in that blues scale.

Example 26: Blues Solo

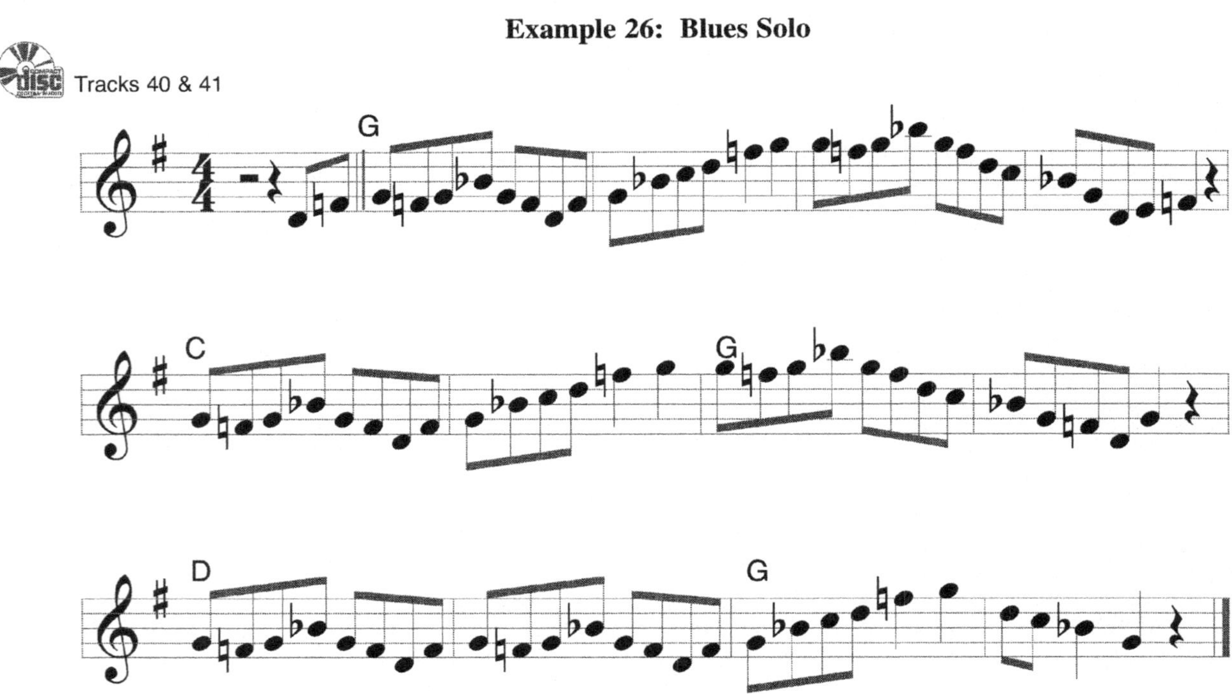

Improvising Strategy Two: Changing Scales With the Chords

Until now, we have ignored changing chords and simply played in the "home" scale. This approach is especially useful when you are unsure of the progression. As developing improvisers, it's now time to start dealing with each chord as it appears in a progression.

Here is a simple progression in letters and numbers:

        D D G G   1 1 4 4

        A A D D   5 5 1 1

We need to know the D, G and A major scales and arpeggios in order to play with this approach. In the next solo, the notes in the first two measures come from the D scale, the next two, G, etc.

Example 27: Changing Chords

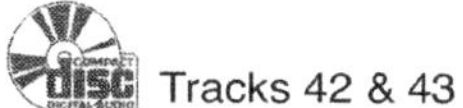

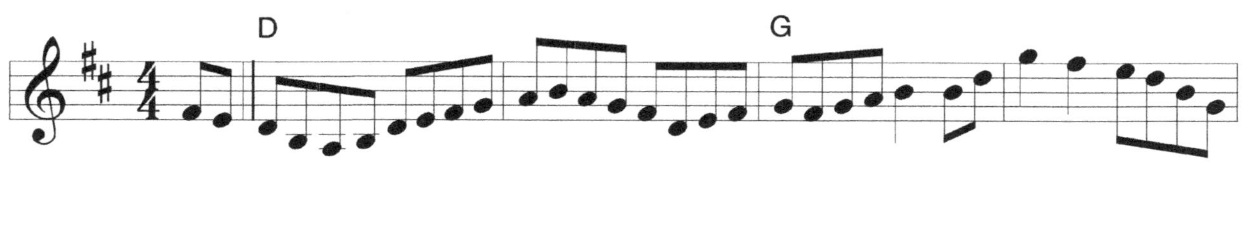

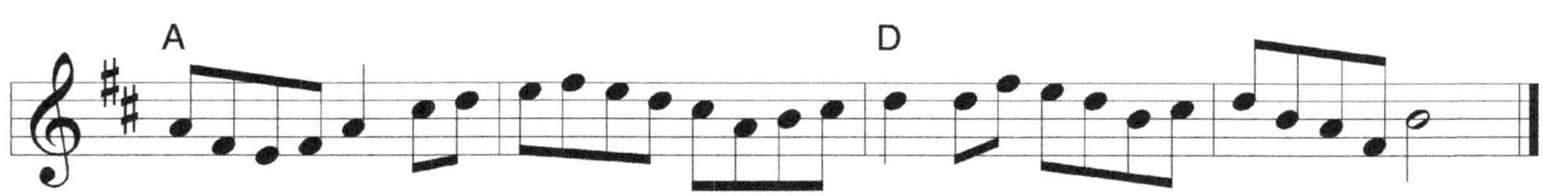

We have to know the progression of the song to play with this approach. With this approach you can play songs that move beyond a simple 1, 4, 5 progression. Songs such as "San Antonio Rose," "Right or Wrong," "Old Fashioned Love," and "Dixie Blues" require this chord-by-chord approach. Even a simple song like "Take Me Back to Tulsa" requires this approach due to the long three measure 5 chord.

Joe's Soloing Rule #4   Change major scales to fit each chord in the song

To learn soloing, Bob Wills' hot electric mandolin player, Tiny Moore, suggested beginning on the 1, 3, or 5 note of the first chord. The soloist should then "aim" to land on a 1, 3, or 5 of the next chord. The next progression is a 6-2-5-1 type in which the solo changes scales for each chord and begins each new chord with a 1 note. Western Swing songs that have this type progression include "Anytime," "Right or Wrong" and "Ragged But Right, "and the jazz standard "Sweet Georgia Brown."

Example 28: Circle 1

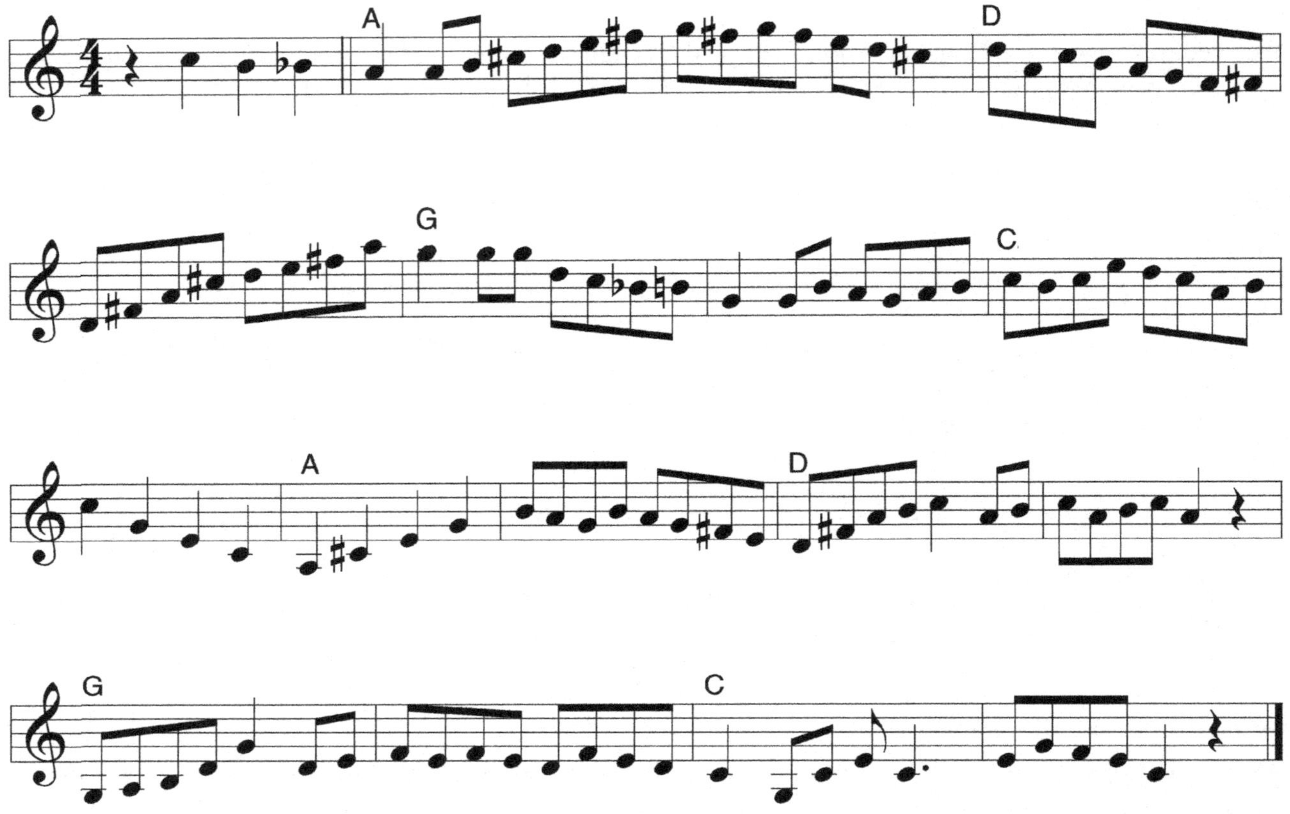

The solo in Example 29 uses the same idea but it starts on different notes (1, 3 or 5) for each chord.

Example 29: Circle 2

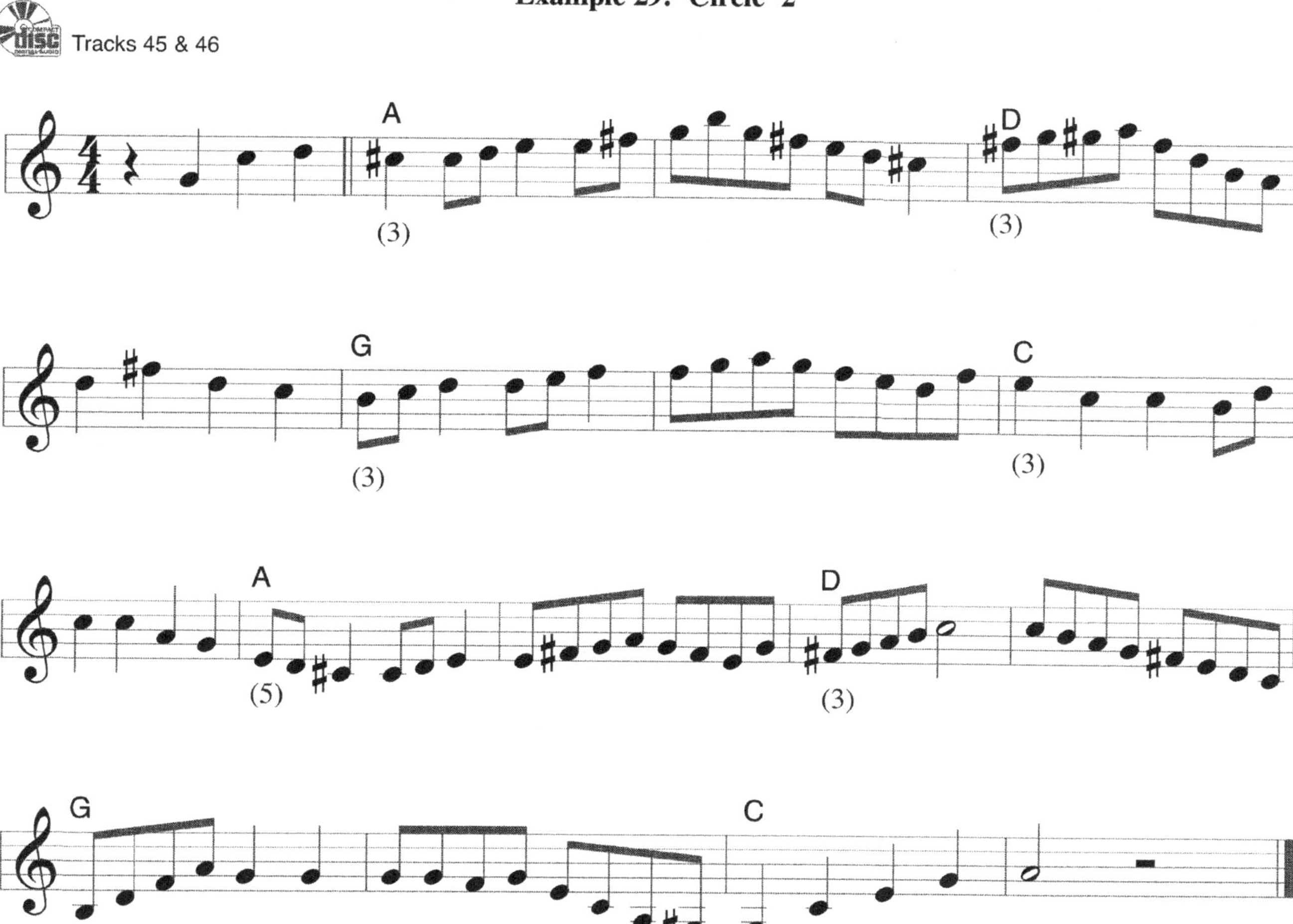

More Soloing Ideas

The concepts presented to this point will serve a developing soloist well. Study them before moving on. The list of possible ideas and approaches is endless. This section presents some popular swing techniques and sounds. Try adding these ideas into your own solos.

Tiny Moore once said that these kinds of ideas should be learned one by one until the concept is familiar and comfortable. If, for instance, you decide to concentrate on the first concept presented here, you should try to use it constantly until it is second nature. Although the musicians around you may tire of hearing the flat 7 note every time the music moves from 1 to 4, you have to use the idea a thousand times before you can call it your own. Then you will be ready to try a new idea and your improvising possibilities expand with every new concept!

Connecting Chords - the Flat 7 Note

The flat 7 is a very powerful note we learned to use in the blues scale. It can also be used to help connect one chord to another. A flat 7 note added to the 1, 3, and 5 notes of a major chord results in a dominant chord. There are many types of chords in the dominant family. The chord that consists of 1, 3, 5, and flat 7 is typical called a "seventh chord." A7 and E7 are examples. Do not confuse this chord with a Major 7 chord, which spells 1, 3, 5, and 7 and is a major, not a dominant, chord.

If you know where the flat 7 note is, you can add it to the major arpeggio to get a dominant 7 arpeggio. Notice that the flatted 7 note is a whole step below the "one" note of a scale. Therefore in G, it is F, in A it is G, etc.

We can use the flat 7 note in two places in a 1 4 5 type chord progression. In the key of A, we can use it to help us move from the A chord to the D chord (1 to 4) and from the E chord to the A chord (5 to 1).

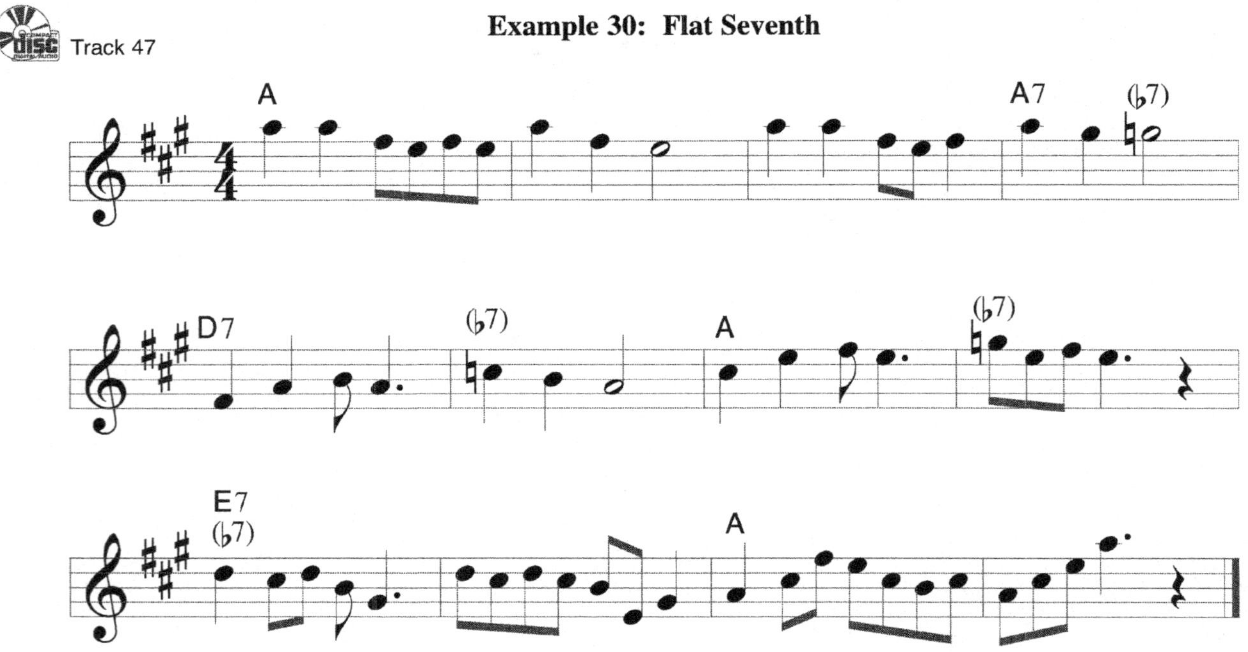

The Major 7th

The major 7th is simply the seventh note of the major scale. The dominant 7th we learned about above is the flatted seventh. The major seventh is often used in the major seventh chord which spells 1 3 5 7. This mellow sounding chord is used in western swing music primarily as a passing chord held only for one or two beats. As a note in a solo however, it can be an ear-catching surprise. Here are two "Gimblesque" major 7 licks.

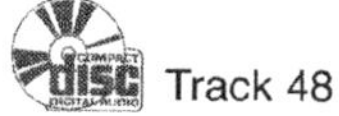
Track 48

Example 31: Major 7th

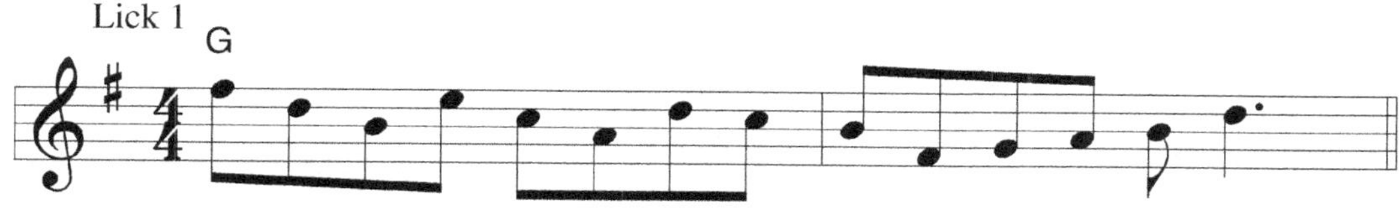

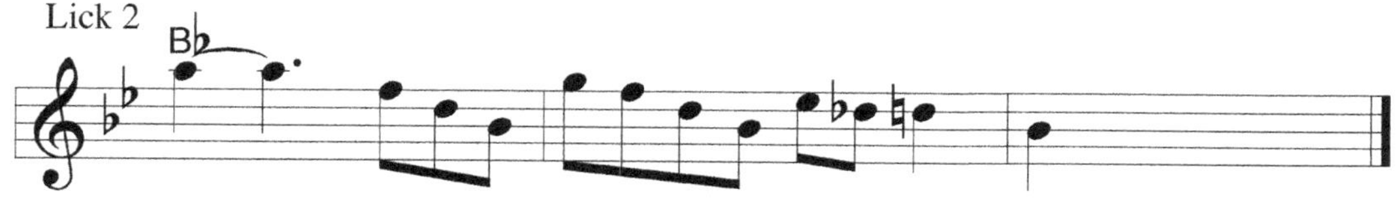

The Ninth

The ninth is a popular sound in swing. The ninth tone of the scale is also the second. In G, the scale looks like this:

G A B C D E F# G A B C

1 2 3 4 5 6 7 8 9 10 11

When a ninth is added to a major chord triad, the result is a major chord and is called a G add 9 or sometimes, G2. When the ninth is added to a Major 7 chord, the result is a Major 9 which spells:

1 3 5 7 9

The ninth chord is a dominant chord and spells 1 3 5 ♭7 9. The result is a slightly more colorful dominant chord which serves the same function as the regular dominant seventh (1 3 5 ♭7.) These chords are interchangeable.

Example 32: The Ninth

Track 49

The Sixth

The Sixth chord is a major chord that spells 1 3 5 6. Fiddlers often add the sixth note over a major chord for a "Hot" or "Swing" sound. The sixth note also appears in a Major 6th chord which spells 1 3 5 6 7. This note can also be used in a dominant situation where it is called the 13th. This is especially true if it is used in a run of notes which include the $\flat$7, 9 or 11. The 13th chord spells 1 3 5 $\flat$7 9 (11) 13. Gimble is fond of beginning a solo with a series of 6th notes.

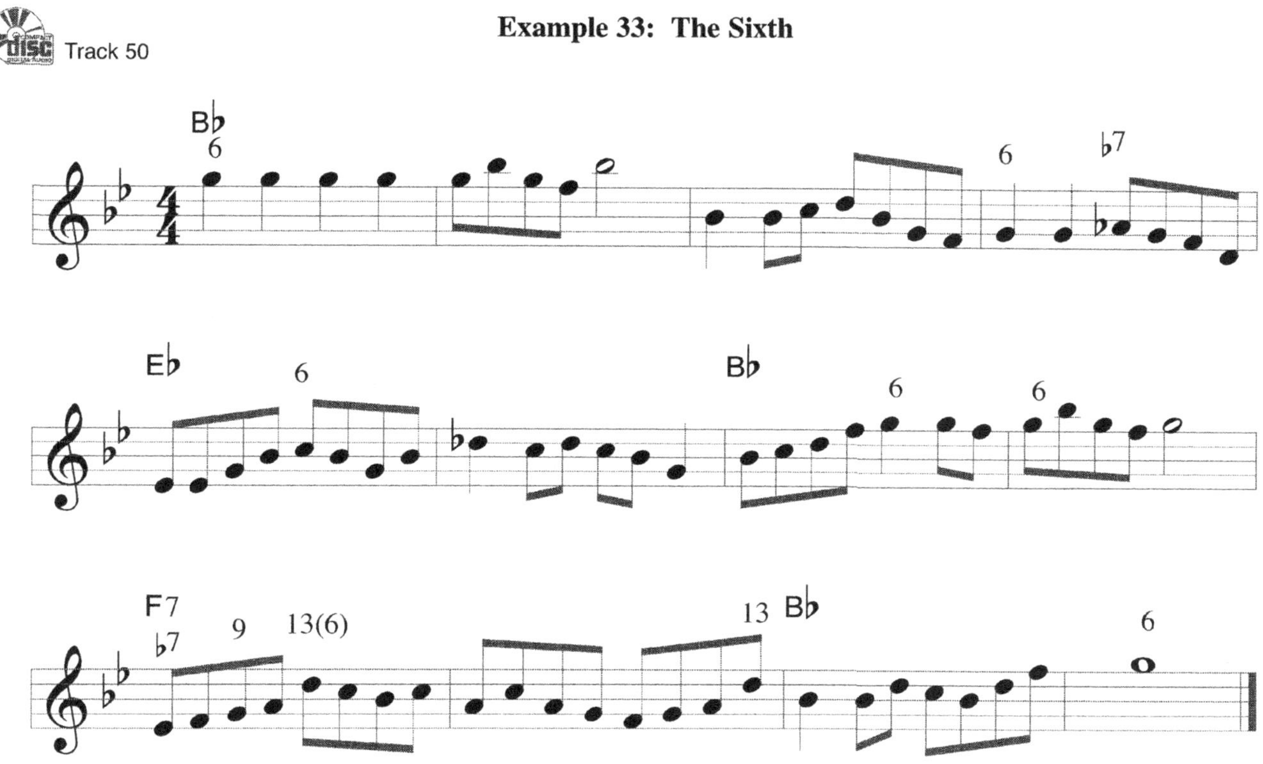

Example 33: The Sixth

Track 50

Shape Licks

Some licks or phrases form shapes or patterns on the fingerboard when they are played. Silently move your fingers through the shape 1 pattern without bowing. Notice that the 1-3 fingering remains the same throughout the lick. Try the three licks built on this shape. These licks can be played in C simply by moving over one set of strings (start lick 1 on a D note on the A string.)

Shape 2 is a lick built on a major 9 arpeggio. The chord numbers of the lick are: 3 5 7 9 1. It also acts like a surrounding figure (see Example 40.)

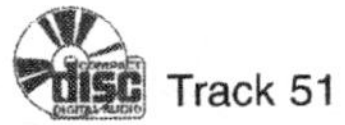

Example 34: Shape Licks

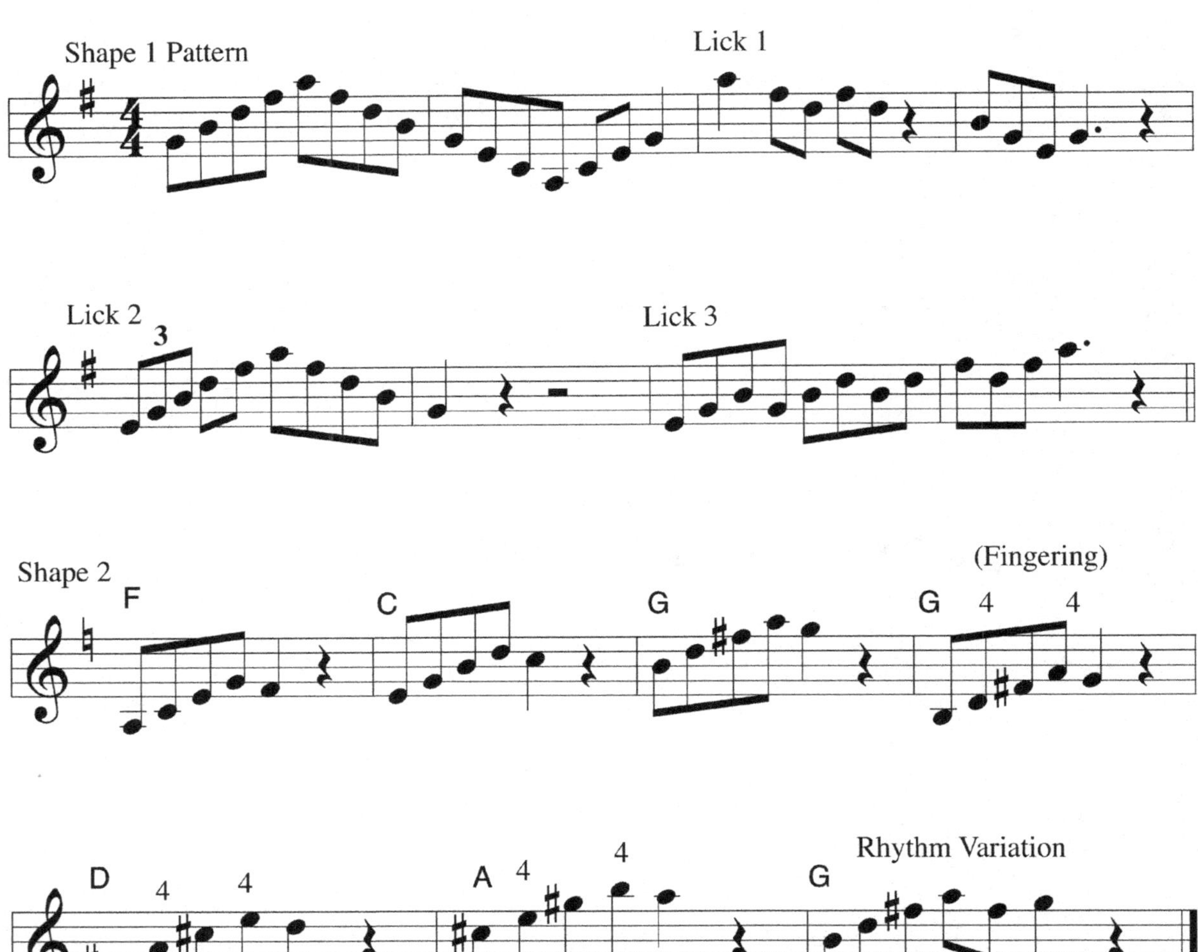

36

Quotes

Quoting in music refers to the practice of inserting part of a well known melody into your solo. Quotes generally get a smile or laugh from listeners and fellow musicians. Simple, short quotes may be used over a measure or two of a single chord. Longer quotes may be played over entire sections of a tune though you risk wearing out the idea. Short, recognizable quotes are probably best. This idea will be demonstrated in the "Putting it All Together" section.

Diminished Runs

The diminished scale is built on an alternating half step, whole step pattern. Since diminished scale use is often limited to one or two beats, the diminished arpeggio works well. The diminished arpeggio makes an easily memorized pattern on the fingerboard. The diminished arpeggio contains four notes. Each of these four notes can be the root of the scale. Therefore, Exercise 1 can be B♭, C♯, E and G diminished arpeggios. Exercise 2 can be B, D, F and G♯. Exercise 3 can be C, D♯, F♯ and A. So, in three scales, we have covered all 12 keys.

There are two fingerings shown for each arpeggio. The first is shape driven and moves through several positions. The second is in first position only.

 Track 52

Example 35: Diminished Scale and Arpeggio

G, B♭, C♯ & E Diminished Scale

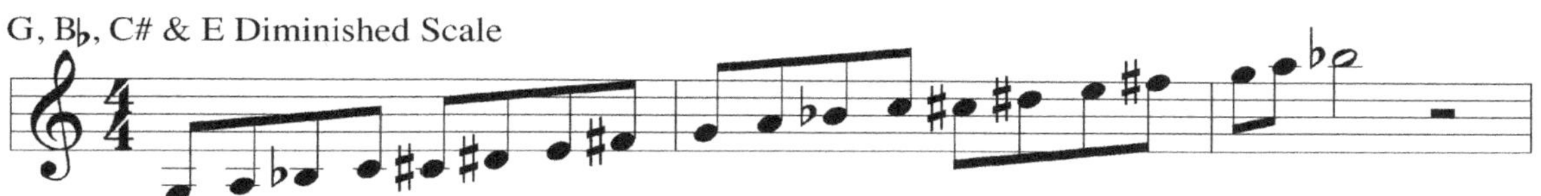

Exercise 1
G, B♭, C♯ & E Arpeggio

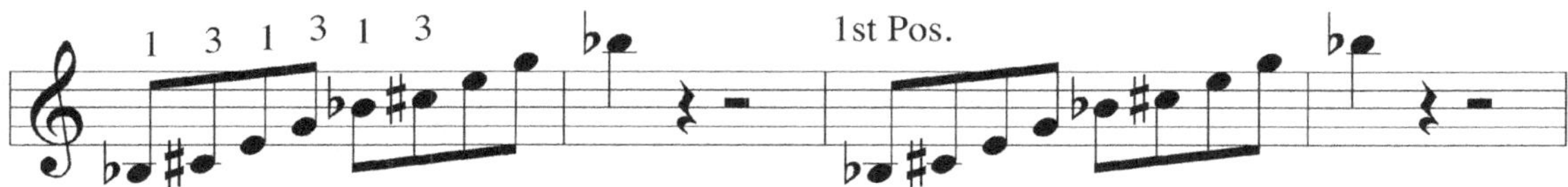

Exercise 2
G♯, B, D & F♯ Arpeggio

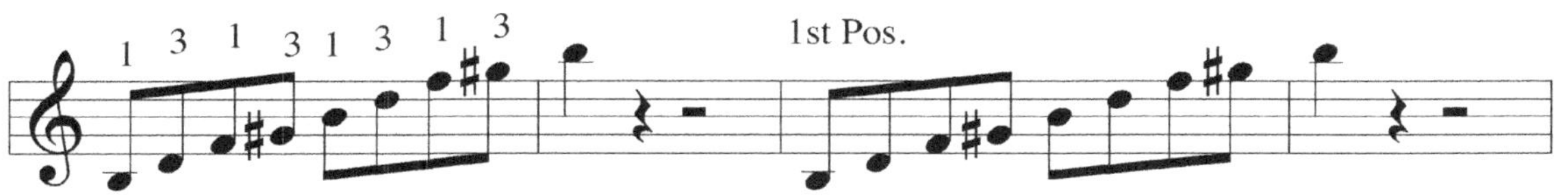

Exercise 3
A, C, D♯ & F♯ Arpeggio

1st Pos.

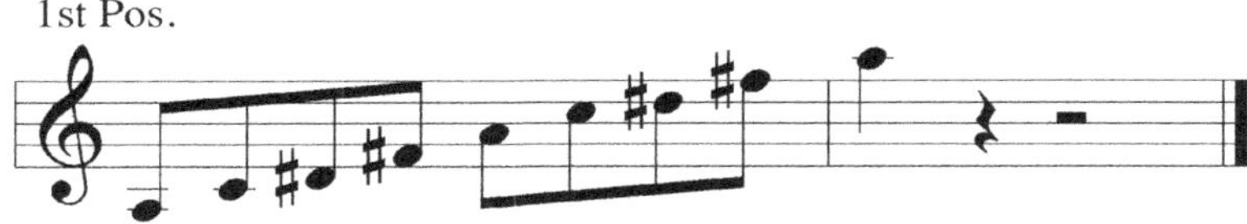

Here are two common ways diminished scales and arpeggios are used:

The diminished chord, arpeggio and scale can all be used as a connection between 4 and 1 chord. The correct diminished scale is 1/2 step above the chord for which you are substituting. For a D7 chord use a D♯ diminished.

Substitution for a dominant chord. The 7♭9 chord and a diminished chord share the same notes and are interchangeable. G7♭9 contains G B D F G♯. G♯ dim contains G♯ B F D.

The example includes both uses.

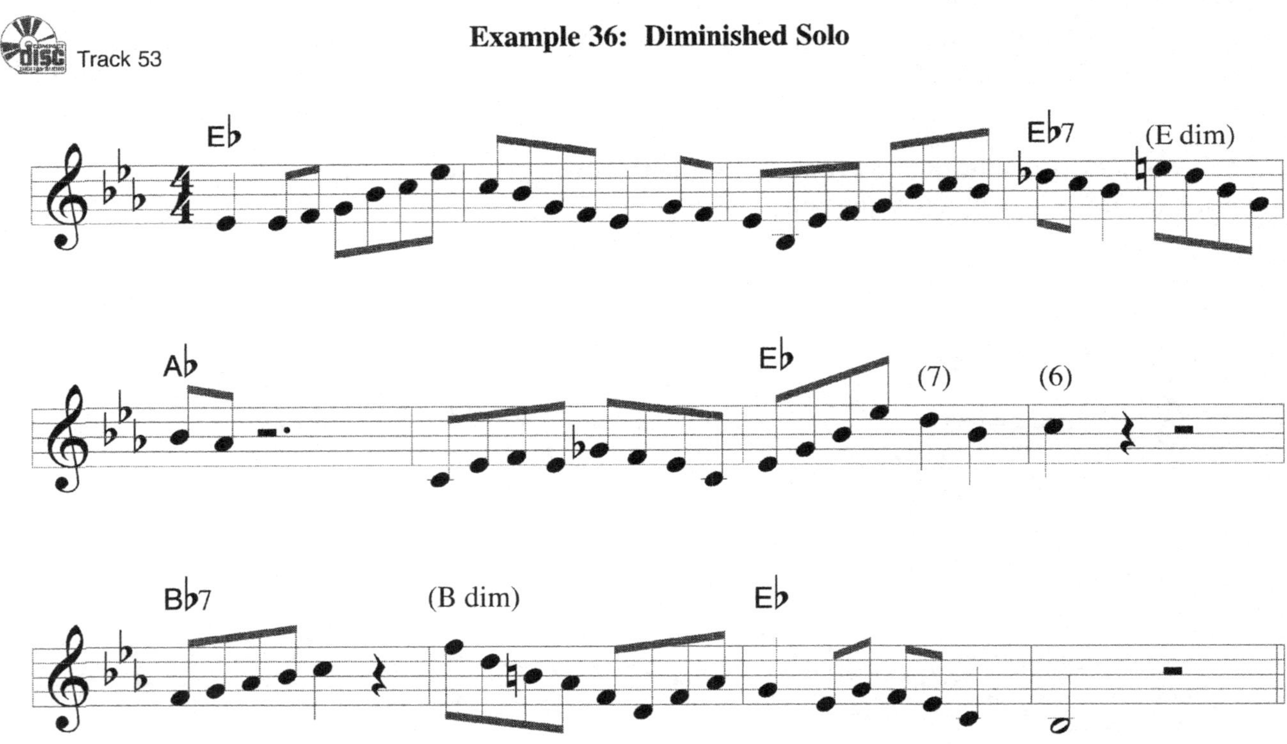

Augmented Runs

A whole tone scale is typically used to solo over an augmented chord (1, 3, ♯5) or augmented 7th chord (1, 3, ♯5, ♭7). They can also be used over dominant 7 chords to imply the augmented sound. A whole tone scale contains no half steps and also makes a pattern on the fingerboard. Since this scale is made from every other note, there are only two whole tone scales:

G A B   C♯ D♯ F   G etc. fits chords with these roots.

G♯ B♭ C   D E F♯ G♯ etc. fits chord with these roots.

Example 37: Augmented Scales

Track 54

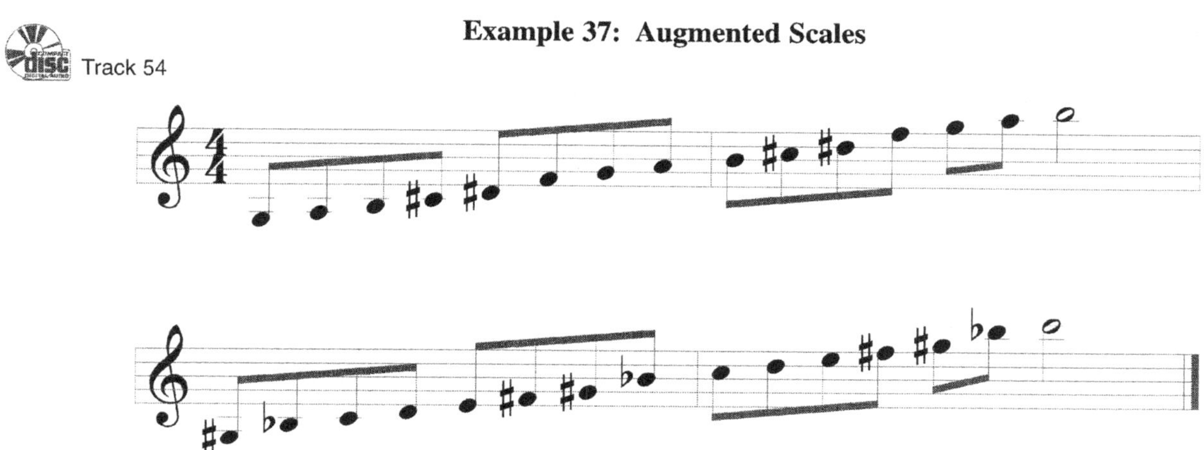

Like the diminished, augmented runs can be used to connect 1 to 4 chords and 5 to 1 chords.

Use the whole tone scale that contains the note naming chord you are substituting. For G7, use a G augmented or a G whole tone scale. You can substitute for the entire time of the chord or some smaller length of time.

Example 38: Augmented Solo

Track 55

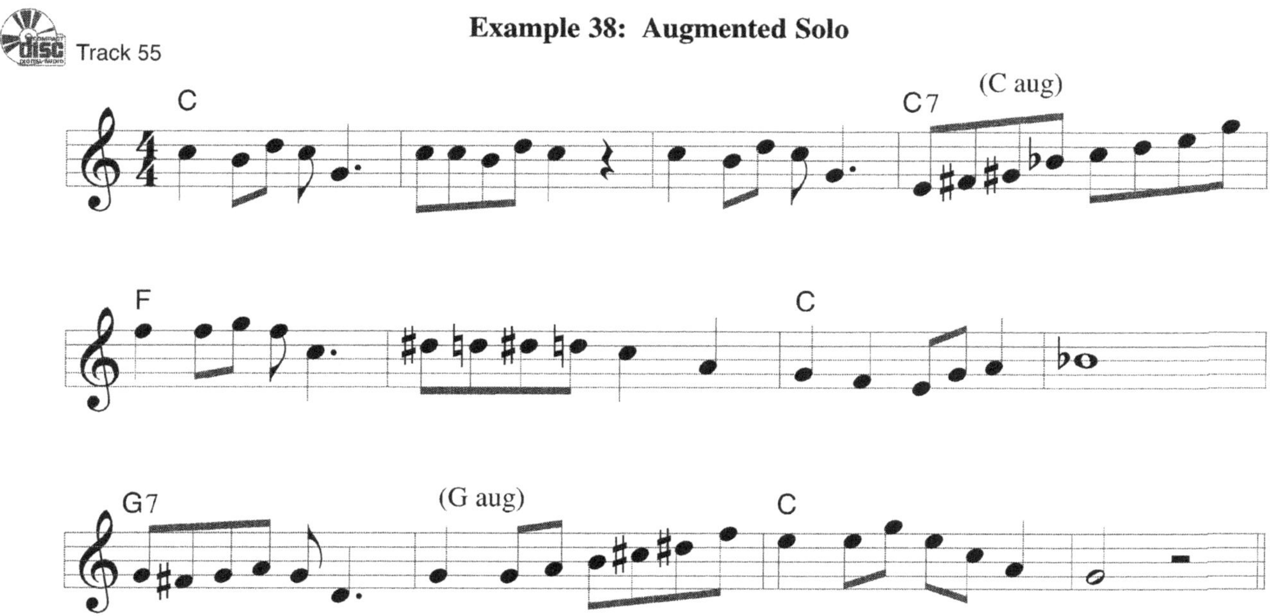

Chord Substitution

The jazz practice of chord substitution can be very rewarding, but complex. Here is a popular idea from this vast field.

For a dominant chord, substitute a minor chord built on the 5th of the dominant chord. This means for a D7 chord you can think Am, for F7 think Cm, G7 - Dm, etc.

Example 39: Chord Substitution

Track 56

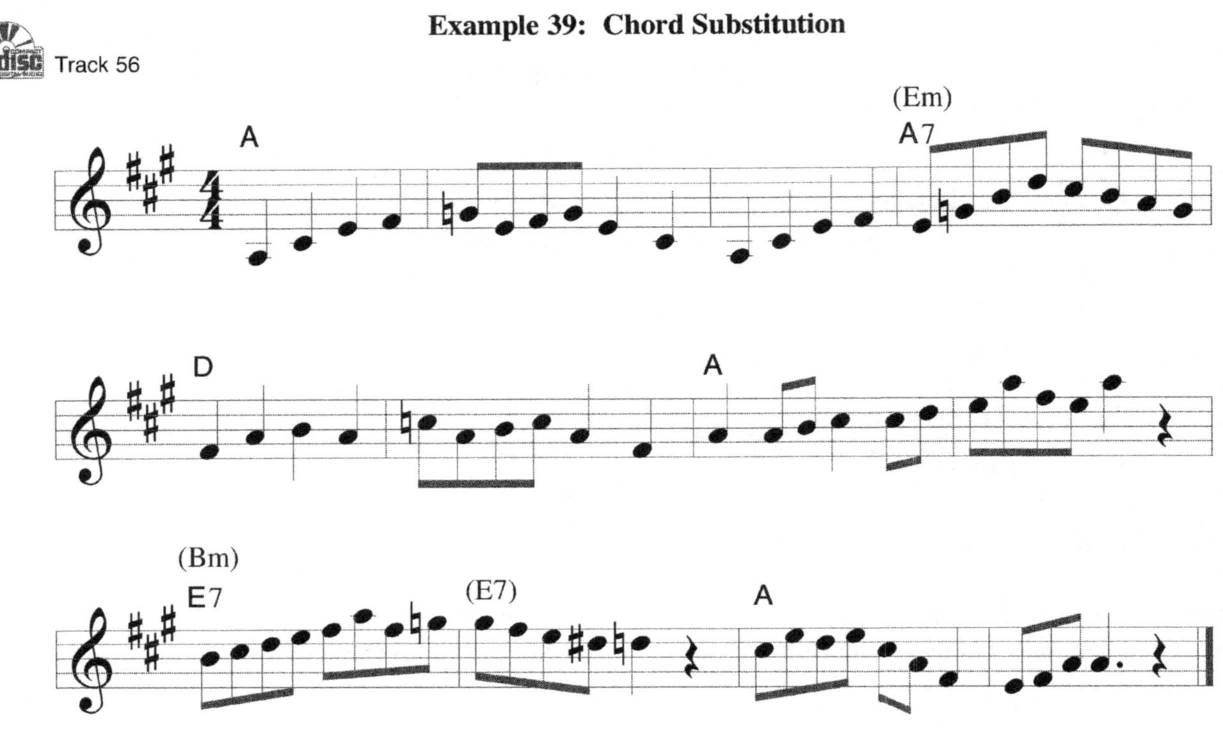

A jazz musician is a juggler who uses harmonies instead of oranges.
- Benny Green

Chord Extension

The basic chord groups including major, minor and dominant can be extended without changing the harmony of the song. Use your ear to see if you like the result in various songs. Here is a selected list.

Major = Major 6, 7 or 9

Minor = Minor 6, 7, 9, 11, or 13

Dominant = 7, 9, 11, 13 and any of these chords with these tones added: $\flat5, \flat9, \sharp9$.

These ideas will be used in the "Putting It All Together" section, and are further discussed in Appendix 4.

The Surrounding Figure

You can create a lick by playing above and below a note before landing on the target note. This can be very effective with arpeggios.

Example 40: Surrounding Figure

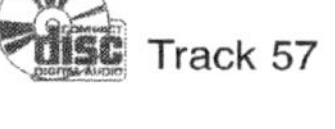

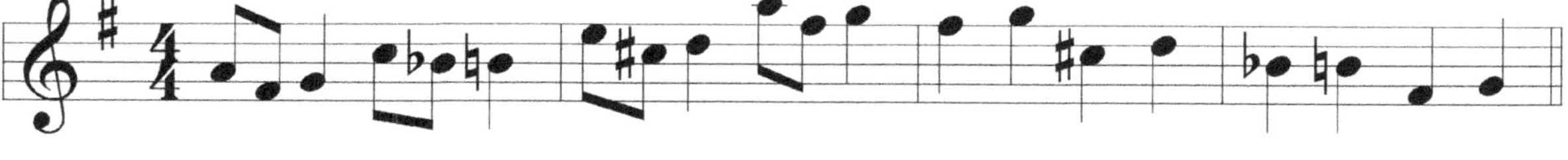

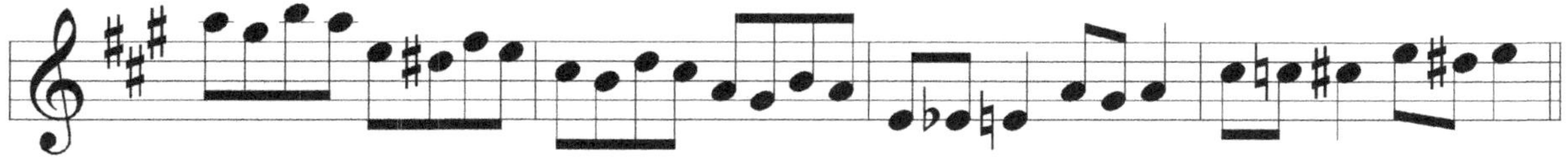

Putting It All Together

Here are some solos that contain many of the ideas discussed previously. The music is marked with references so that you can see "what the soloist is thinking." Steal these licks and transpose them to other keys.

Example 41

Tracks 58 & 59

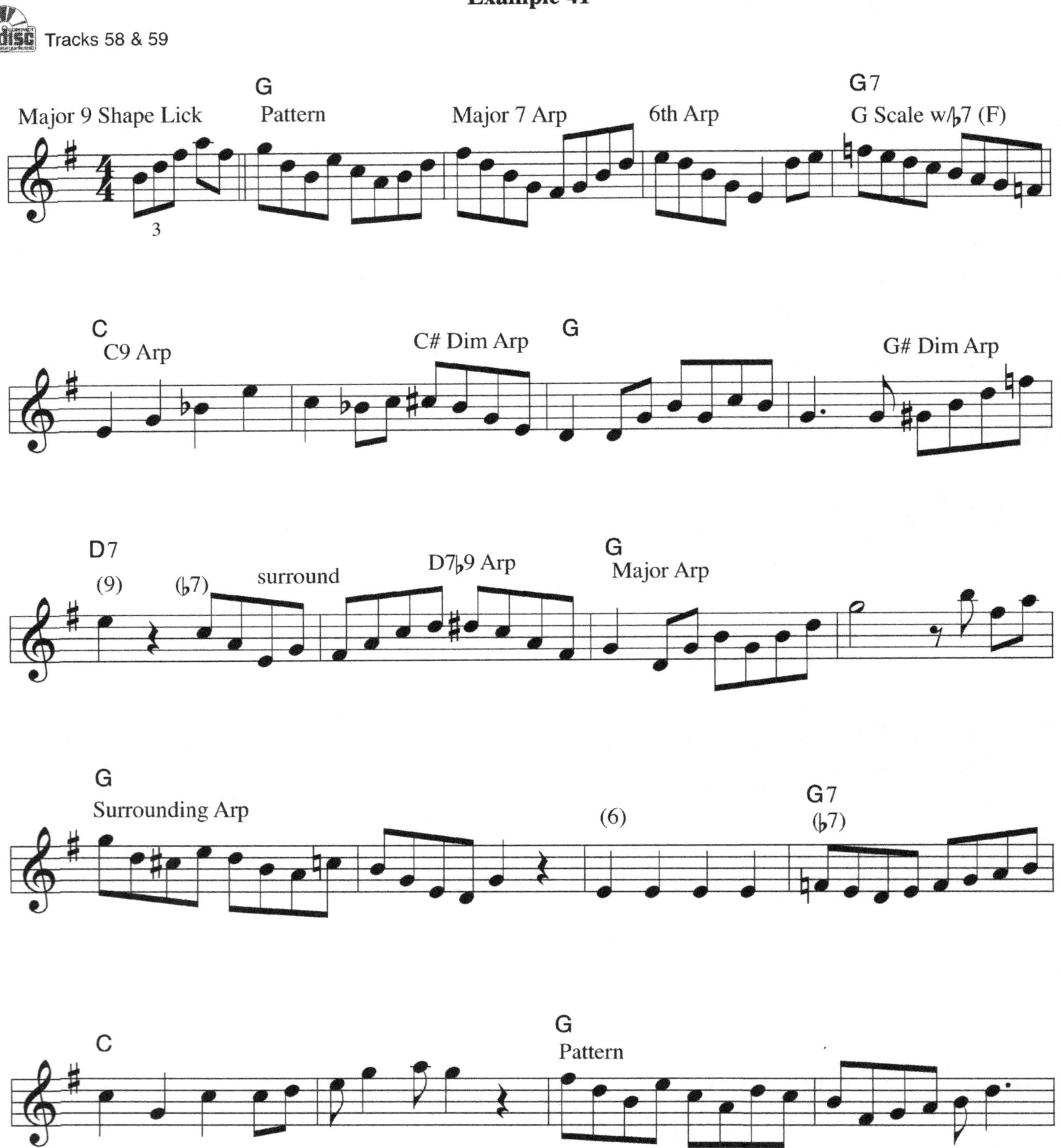

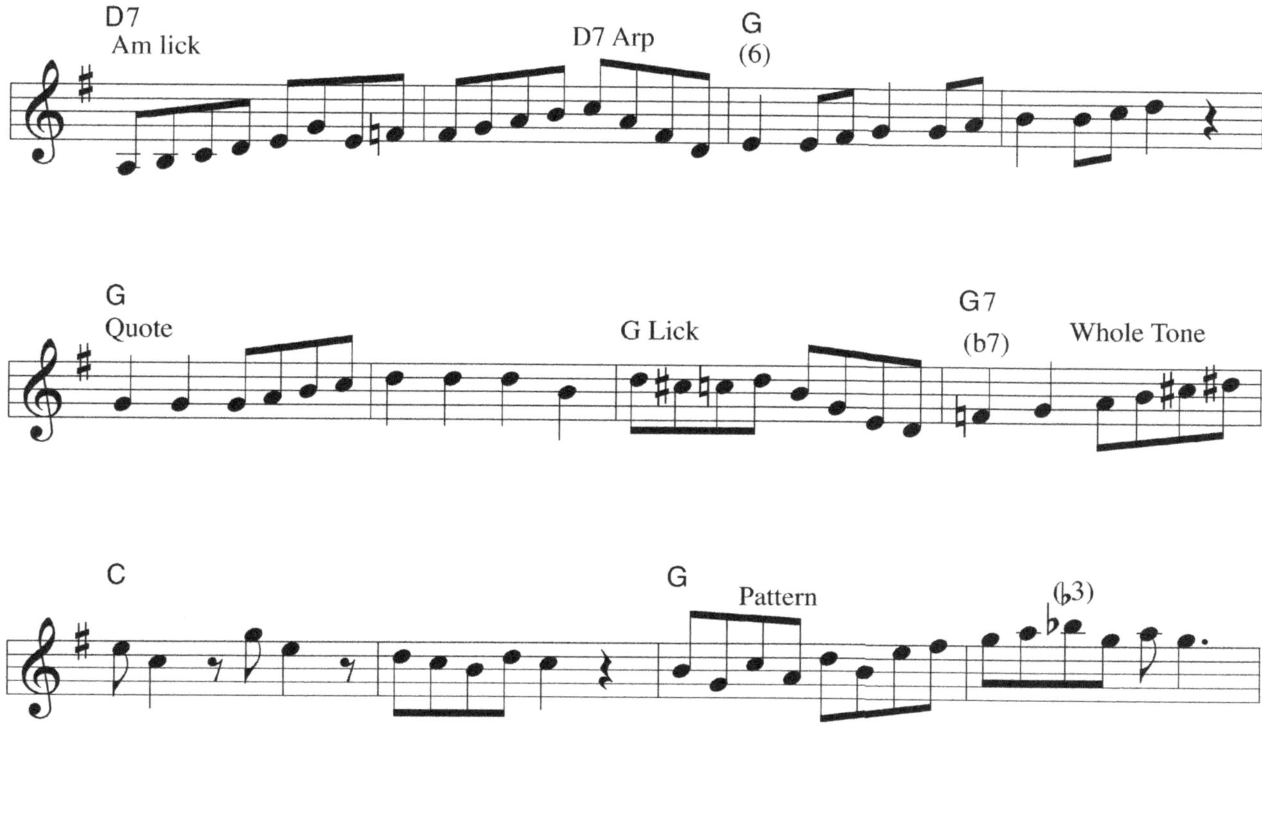

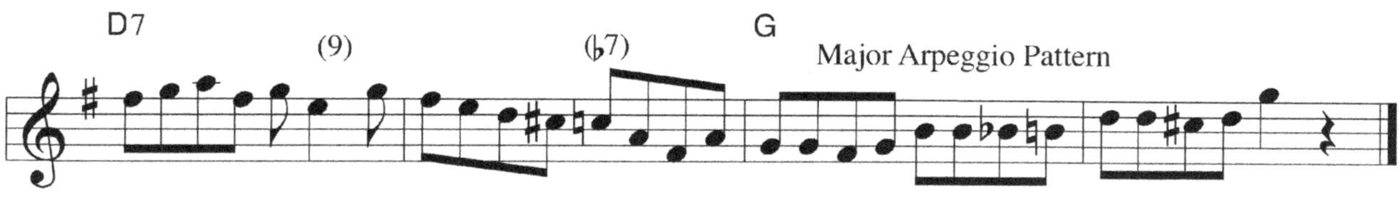

A good composer does not imitate; he steals.
- Igor Stravinsky

Analyzing Recorded Solos

To continue your studies, listen to favorite swing solos and analyze the music. The first staff of the example below is the basic melody to a simple song. The second staff is a stylized interpretation of the melody in the style of early western swing great Cliff Bruner.

Example 42: Bruner 1

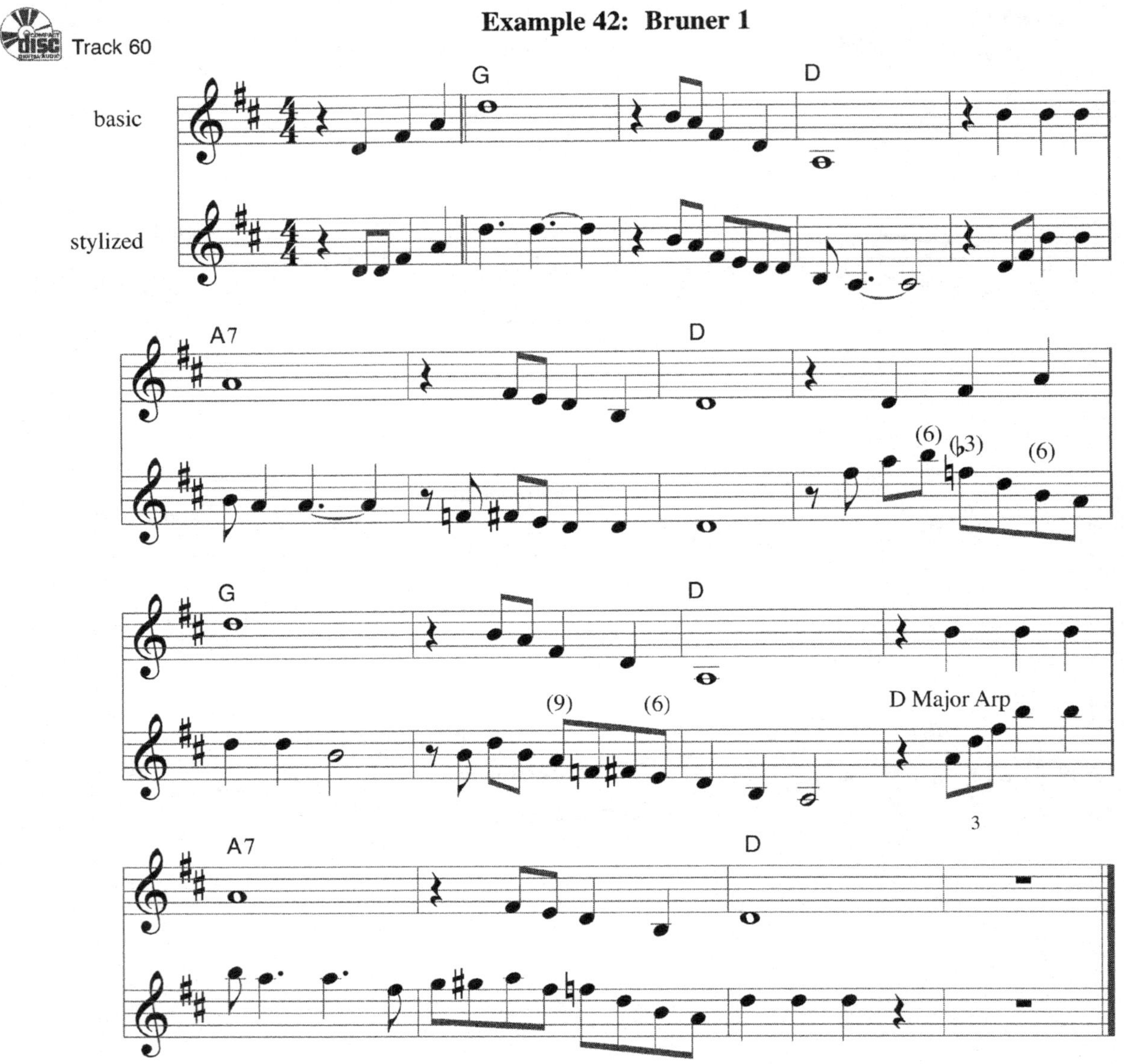

Analysis of Example 42, Stylized Solo

In the first 7 bars, the melody is largely intact, but the rhythm is changed to swing. In measure 8, a hot lick with sixths and a bluesey flatted third lead back to the melody in measure 9. The lick is syncopated, starting on the "and" beat (or up beat) after "one." This syncopated figure is mirrored in measure 10. The triplet D6 arpeggio in measure 12 leads to the "A" melody note in the next measure. The solo ends with a hot lick with lots of chromatic notes in measures 14-15.

Analysis of Example 43, Hot Solo

Several licks in this example should be memorized and used in other songs. The phrase in measure 8 works in a static D situation as well as the D to G situation seen here. The D6 arpeggio in measure 12 is also attractive. In the next example, the solo we just studied is on staff one. The hot solo on staff two is in Bruner's style.

Example 43: Bruner 2

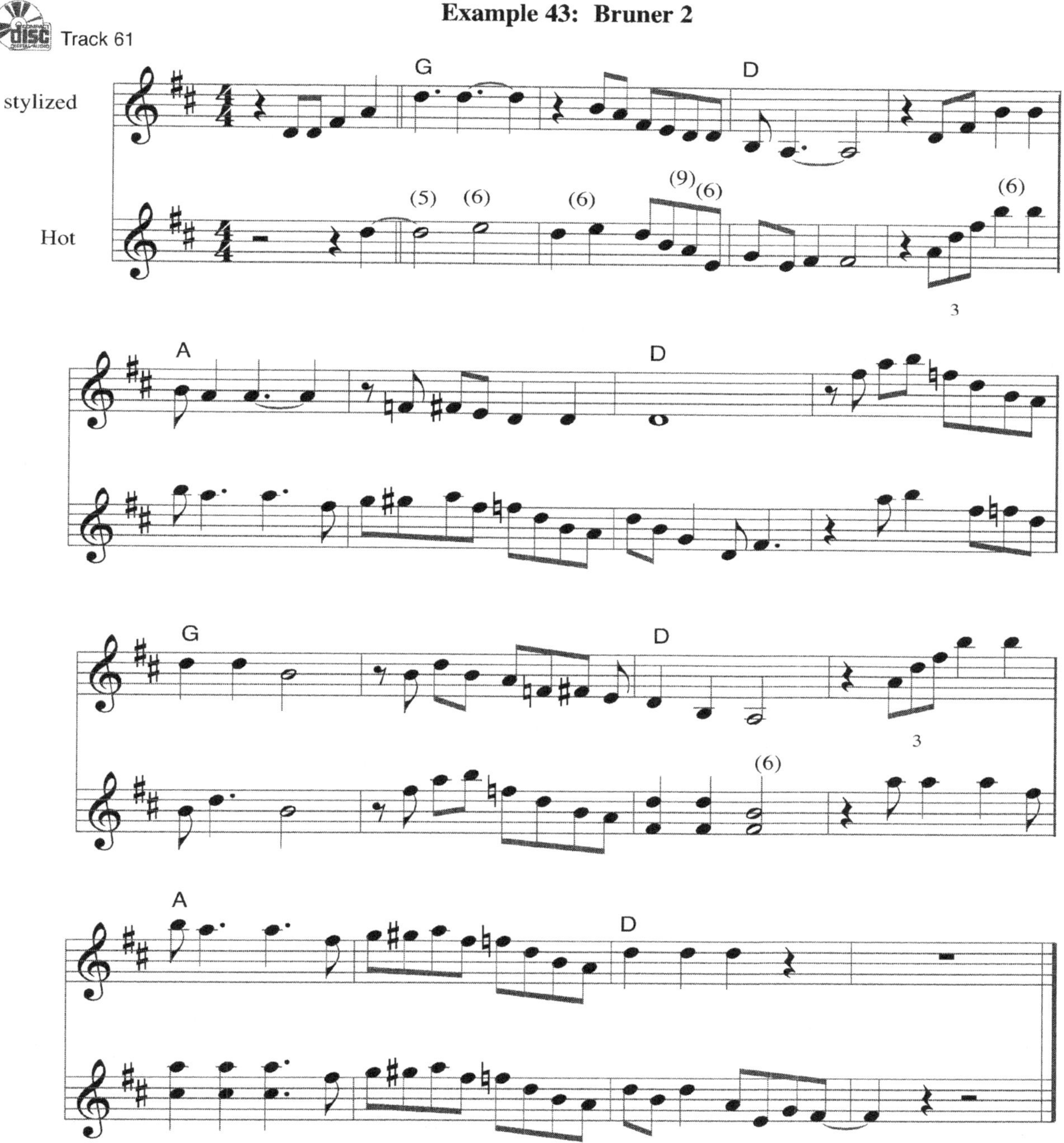

The final tune is an original called "The Mike Richey Special." It contains many of the ideas we have discussed here. The B part of the tune bears a striking resemblance to "The Golden Eagle Hornpipe."

Example 44: The Mike Richey Special.

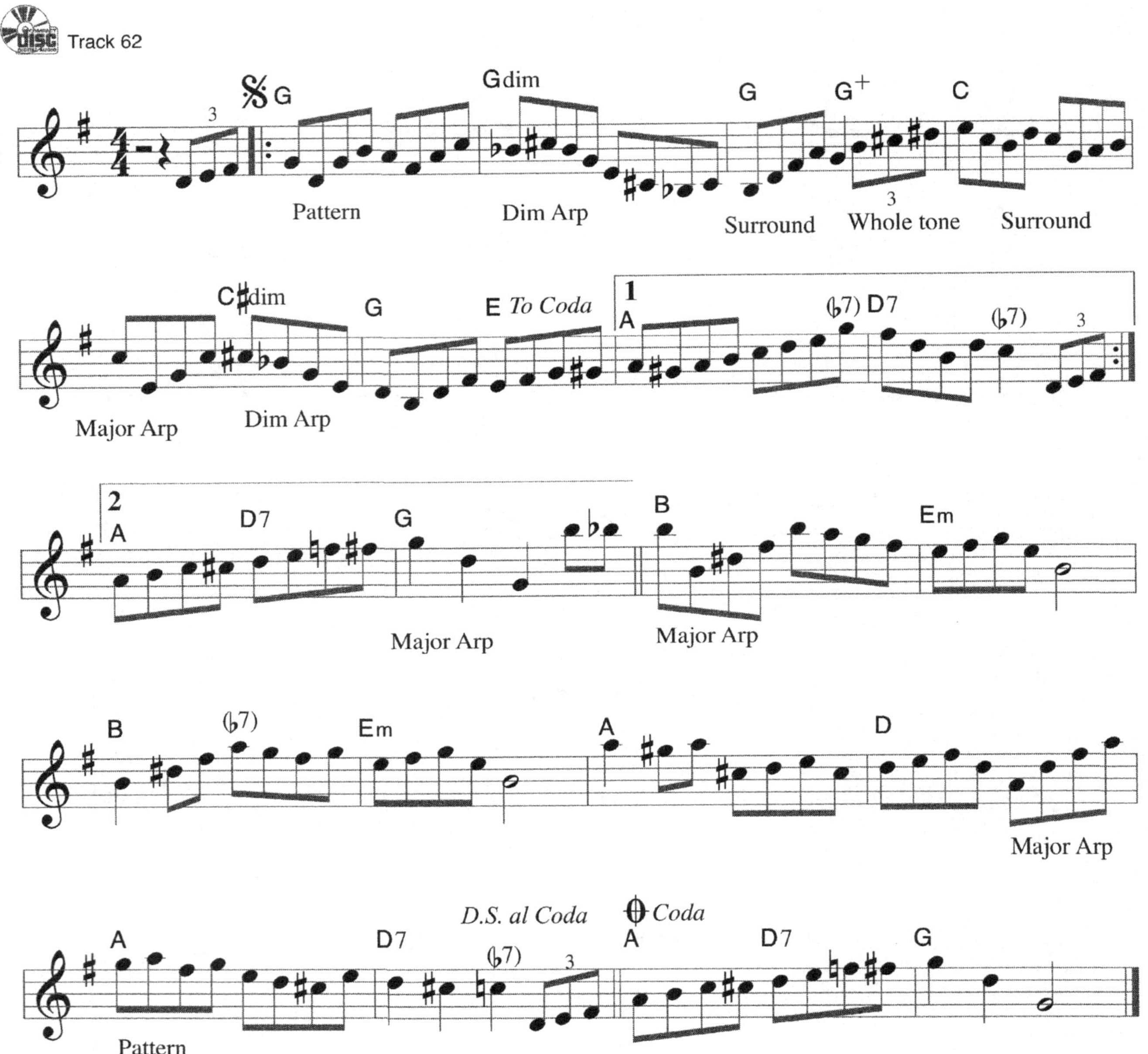

Conclusion

The information in this book may take a long time to soak in. While some ideas may be instantly clear and obvious, others may take years. Tiny Moore suggested taking a single concept (using a flat 7 note to move from a 1 chord to a 4, for example) and using it constantly, in every solo, until you thoroughly understand how and when to use it. Then you can move on to another idea and incorporate it into your solos.

Western Swing is one of the most challenging American country fiddling styles. Because it borrows so much from early jazz, it can be a very complicated music. Do not expect to master the style in a short time. If you love this music, it will be a lifelong pursuit and your personal style will evolve as you incorporate new ideas.

There is nothing more notable in Socrates than that he found time,
when he was an old man, to learn music, and thought it time well spent.
- Michel de Montaigne

Appendix I First Position Major Pentatonic Scales

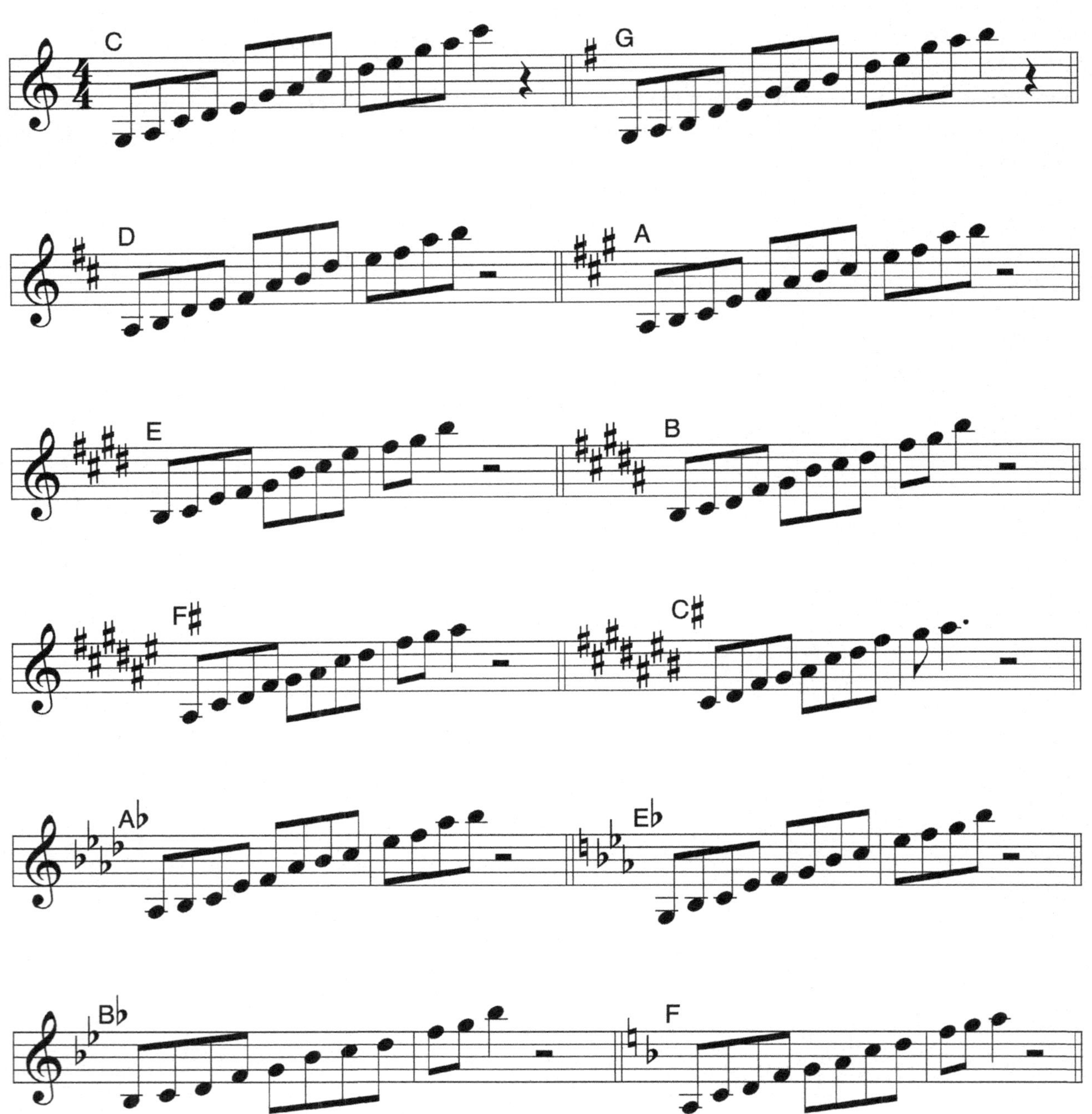

Appendix II First Position Major Scales

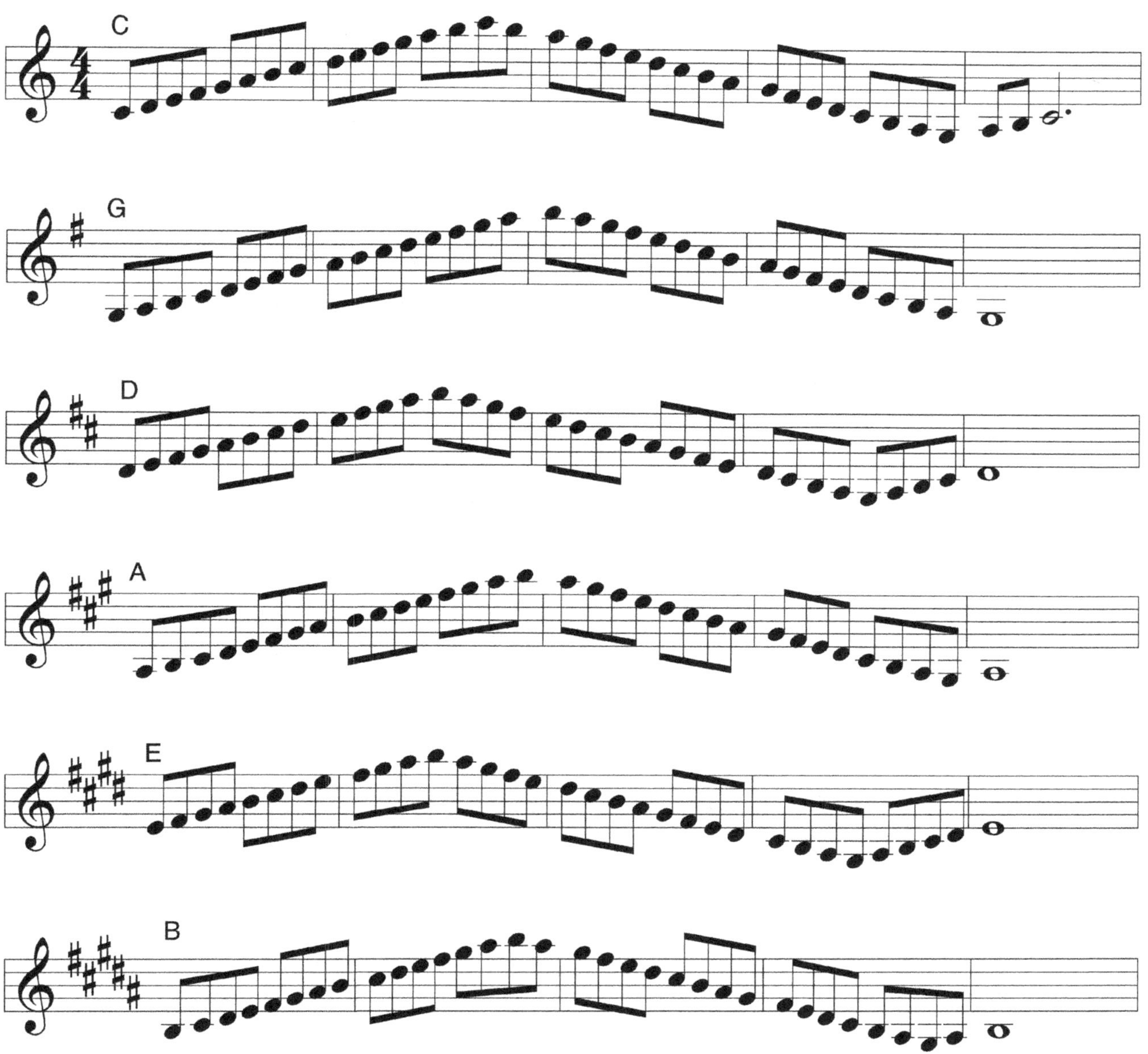

Appendix II First Position Major Scales (con't)

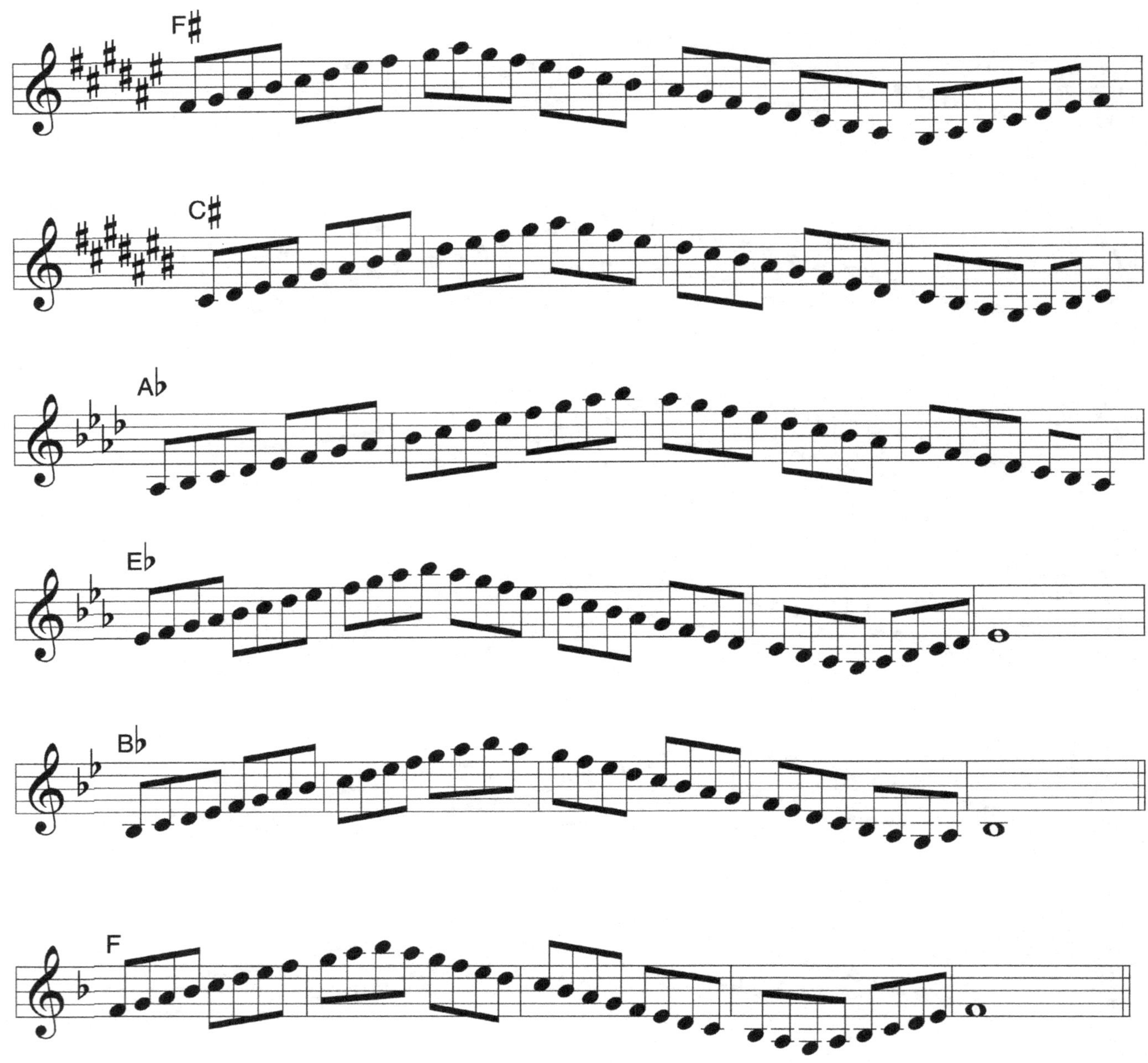

Appendix III First Position Major Arpeggios

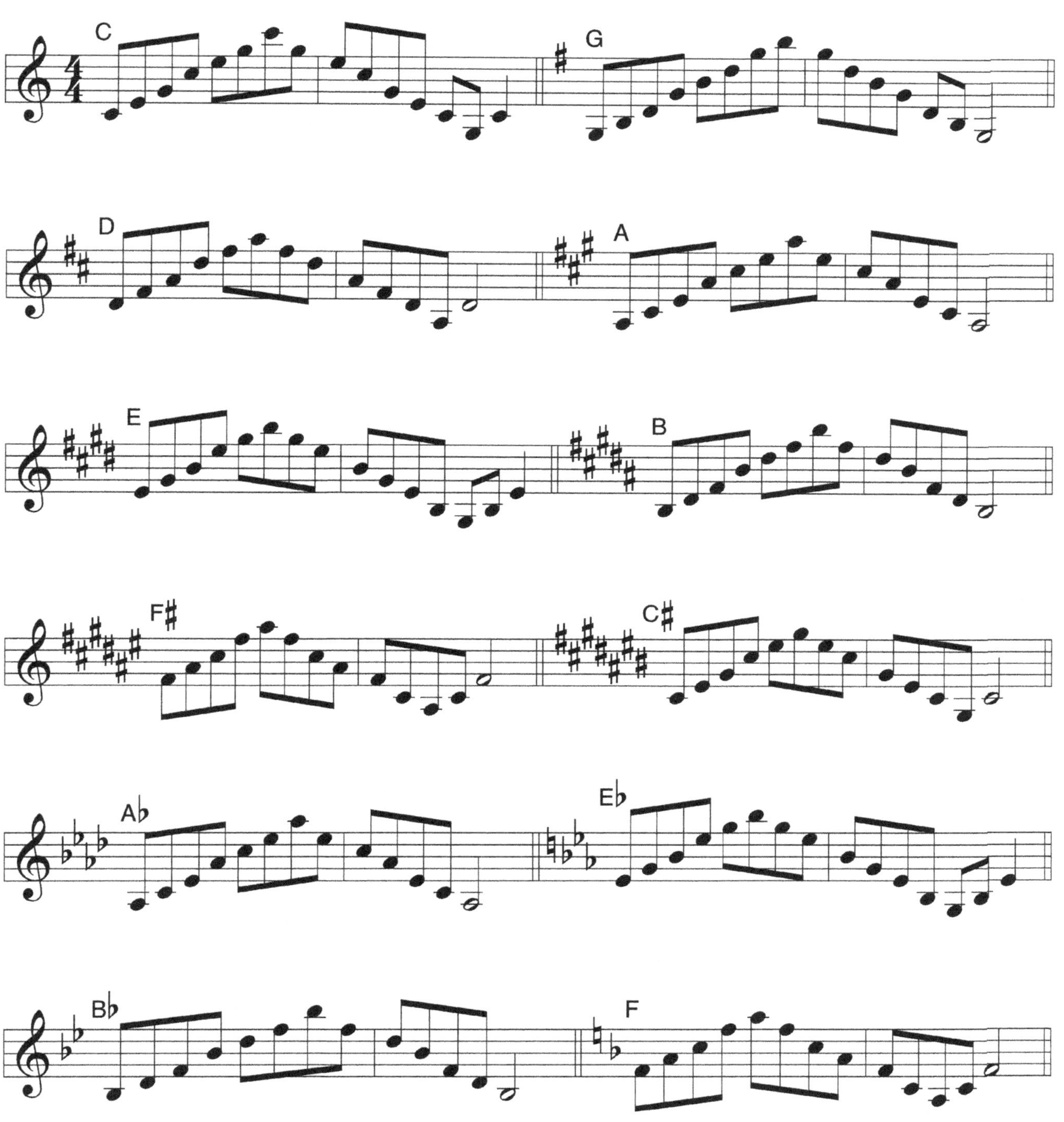

Appendix IV Chords and How They Work

In these examples, the G major scale with be assigned these numbers:

G A B C D E F♯ G A B C D E

1 2 3 4 5 6 7 8 9 10 11 12 13

In this appendix, we will work with four chord families: Major, Minor, Dominant, and Altered. This is a partial list of common chord types. It is by no means complete. I have indicated some of the more common swing chords.

Major - Consists of the first, third and fifth note of the major scale (in the key of G: G B D). Other major chord types start with 1, 3, 5 and then add other notes.

6th	1	3	5	6	Very common in Swing
Major 7	1	3	5	7	
Major 9	1	3	5	7	9

Minor - Consists of the first, flatted third and fifth note of the scale. In G: G B♭ D. Other minor chord types are formed when other notes are added to the 1 ♭3 5 triad.

Minor 6	1	♭3	5	6
Minor 7	1	♭3	5	♭7
Minor 9	1	♭3	5	♭7 9

Dominant - Consists of the basic major triad plus the flatted 7. This basic dominant chord is often called a "seventh." Other examples are:

7th	1	3	5	♭7	Common in Swing
9th	1	3	5	♭7 9	Common in Swing
11th	1	3	5	♭7 9 11	

Altered - Included in this category are:

Diminished	1	♭3	♭5	♭♭7	Used in Swing
Augmented	1	3	♯5		Used in Swing
Augmented 7th	1	3	♯5	♭7	Used in Swing
Suspended 4	1	4	5		
Suspended 2	1	2	5		

Appendix V Relative Majors and Minors

Relative Major	Relative Minor
C	Am
G	Em
D	Bm
A	F♯m
E	C♯m
B	G♯m
F♯	D♯m
C♯	A♯m
A♭	Fm
E♭	Cm
B♭	Gm
F	Dm

Other Mel Bay Publications by Joe Carr

96899D	25 Great Back-Up Licks for Flatpicking Guitar
95091VX	60 Hot Licks for Bluegrass Mandolin-Video
95101BCD	60 Hot Licks for Western Swing Guitar-Book/CD Set
96847DVD	Banjo Chords-DVD
96849DVD	Baritone Uke Chords-DVD
95615DVD	Complete Country Guitar-DVD
96851DVD	Dulcimer Chord -DVD
99973BCD	First Lessons Flatpicking Guitar-Book/CD Set
99973SET	First Lessons Flatpicking Guitar-Book+CD+DVD
93268DP	Fun with the Banjo-Book+DVD
93268DVD	Fun with the Banjo-DVD
93266DVD	Fun with the Baritone Uke-DVD
93262DVD	Fun with the Guitar-DVD
93258DP	Fun with the Mandolin-Book+DVD
93258DVD	Fun with the Mandolin-DVD
93260DVD	Fun with the Tenor Banjo-DVD
93270DP	Fun with the Ukulele-Book+DVD
93270DVD	Fun with the Ukulele-DVD
20290BCD	Getting Into Bluegrass Guitar: A Crash Course into Bluegrass and Flatpicking Guitar Styles-Book/CD Set
20288BCD	Getting Into Country Guitar-Book/CD Set
20553BCD	Great Mandolin Picking Tunes-Book/CD Set
95659DVD	Guitar Chords Encyclopedia-DVD
20823BCD	International Favorites for Mandolin-Book/CD Set
96846DVD	Mandolin Chords DVD
20287	Mandolin Wall Chart
95998DVD	Super Mandolin Picking Techniques-DVD
96850DVD	Tenor Banjo Chords-DVD
98404BCD	Texas Fiddle Favorites for Mandolin-Book/CD Set
96848DVD	Uke Chords-DVD
94906BCD	Western Swing Guitar Styles-Book/CD Set

Notes

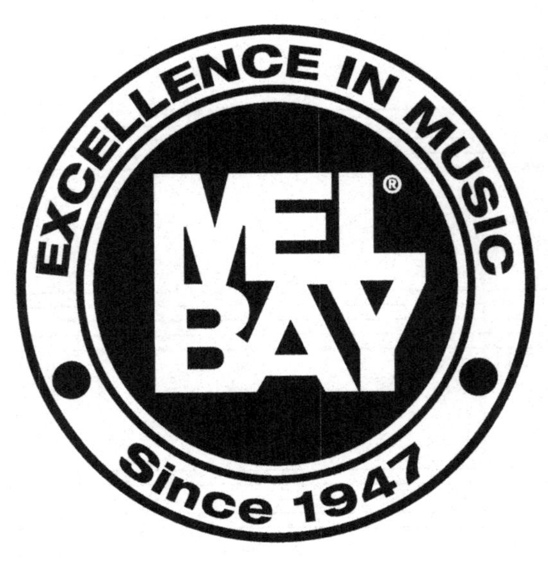

WWW.MELBAY.COM

Made in the USA
Columbia, SC
24 September 2020